BABIES
NEED BOOKS

BABIES NEED BOOKS

by Dorothy Butler

Atheneum   New York   1980

LIBRARY OF CONGRESS CATALOGING IN PUBLICATION DATA

Butler, Dorothy, date
Babies need books.

Includes bibliographies.

1. Infants—Books and reading. 2. Books and reading
for children. 3. Children's literature—Bibliography.
I. Title.
Z1037.A1B87   010   80-14027

Contents

For Roy

It must be rare to have a typist who corrects one's grammar and punctuation, questions one's judgement from time to time, and even identifies one's literary lapses. This I have had in the person of my daughter Christine who, typing on my dining table with her two sons playing about her feet, has given me constant support, companionship and encouragement.

To Chris, and to the rest of my forbearing and good-humored family, my love and gratitude.

My formal thanks are due to E. P. Dutton for permission to use lines from A. A. Milne's poem "When I Was One" from *Now We Are Six* as headings for Chapters 3, 4, 5 and 6; and to G. P. Putnam's Sons for the poem "Too Little to Look?" by Dorothy Aldis for the headings to Chapter 2. The poem is reprinted from *Everything and Anything* by permission of the publishers, Copyright 1925, 1926, 1927 by Dorothy Aldis; renewed.

D.B.

Introduction

I believe that books should play a prominent part in children's lives from babyhood; that access to books, through parents and other adults, greatly increases a child's chances of becoming a happy and involved human being.

The dedicated involvement of parents and other adults is, of course, an essential part of the process. Without the help of adults, a baby or small child has no chance at all of discovering books, of starting on the road to that unique association with the printed word which the mature reader knows and loves.

It is in the hope of persuading parents and others of the truth of this proposition that I have written this book. I want it to be of use to parents in much the same way as a car manual is of use to the motorist who aspires to give personal care and attention to his vehicle.

Fortunately, this need not mean encumbering parents with yet another onerous duty. Children's books these days are things of beauty and delight. The adult who becomes convinced that he should share them with his children has presented himself with a passport to fun, quite apart from the opportunity to stay in touch with his children through the years when their minds are daily expanding.

Children are, of course, different from cars. In an extremity, you can hand your car over to the care of an expert mechanic and be reasonably sure that his attention and skill will solve your problems. Delegation does not work so well for the young child. As society is now constituted, no agent seems to be as effective with the very young human being as one loving adult. Two, if possible, but one certainly.

A reassuring truth, in these days of increasing female involvement with the world outside the home, is that quality, not quantity, is the keynote of any relationship. Any two partners profit from a break, and this is as true of parent and child as it is of two adults. Over-exposure to the developing young, however well-loved they be, can lead to irritation (if not desperation!), with all the damaging effects this implies for both parties.

But a note of caution must be struck; if contact-hours are to be reduced, ways must be found for parents and children to experience one another joyfully during the time they are together.

It is my belief that there is no "parents' aid" which can compare with the book in its capacity to establish and maintain a relationship with a child. Its effects extend far beyond the covers of the actual book, and invade every aspect of life. Parents and children who share books come to share the same frame of reference. Incidents in everyday life constantly remind one or the other—or both, simultaneously—of a situation, a character, an action, from a jointly enjoyed book, with all the generation of warmth and well-being that is attendant upon such sharing.

A great deal is written and said these days about the breakdown of communications between adolescents and their parents. All around us we hear adults complaining:

"He never tells us anything."

"She doesn't even want to know what we think about anything."

"Discuss the problem with him? You must be joking!"

In most of these cases, the give-and-take of shared opinion and ideas has never been practiced before adolescence. The only reason some parents ultimately want to talk with their sons and daughters is that a very real problem has arisen. Adolescence is certainly the time for real problems—problems that can't be ignored, concealed, or smoothed over. But all too often, a parent is the very last person to whom the adolescent wants to talk. Not only has the line of communication never been set up, but all sorts of tensions and awkwardness have.

All of this can be avoided by the early forging of relationships, by establishing the habit of verbal give-and-take. This does not mean that problems won't arise. It merely means that the human beings concerned will have ways of coping with difficulties, ways which may lead to the deepening rather than the damaging of relationships.

And books can play a major part in this process. Because by their very nature they are rooted in language, and because language is essential to human communication, and communication is the life blood of relationships, books *matter*.

Well, then: How do we introduce books to babies? Which books? When? There may be some rare individuals who can cope unaided when they decide to adopt a new approach, but most of us are mere mortals, and need help. I well remember my own "groping" days as a young parent. I know that I made mistakes, worried and felt guilty (often about the wrong things), steeled myself to behave in ways that were later revealed as not only useless but potentially damaging . . . and that always, always, in every area of parenthood, I could have used more informed advice than seemed available.

I'm still learning. My grandchildren keep teaching me things about small children that my own children left untaught, not least in the field of language and books. My love for them is tinged with gratitude, and constant wonder.

If this book can offer a little support to adults who are a bit further back on the learning trail in the book field than I am, I shall be pleased.

ABOUT THIS BOOK

I've made Chapter 1 a "Why?" chapter, in case anyone reading this is sceptical of the whole proposition: that is, that involvement with books from babyhood is one of the greatest blessings and benefits that can come to any child.

If you are convinced of this already, and merely seek advice about ways, means and materials, you may prefer to begin with Chapter 2, which plunges into the mechanics of the thing. But read Chapter 1 later, if only to fortify yourself for encounters with sceptical friends.

The Book Lists between the chapters are to be regarded as important sections of the whole. Long lists are very daunting, so I have selected titles with great care. Nothing is included which I have not used myself with babies or small children. I have tried to describe each in such a way that you will understand my reason for suggesting it, and the way in which you might use it.

It goes without saying that there are other books available which might do just as well. I make no apology for including *my* favorite books, and hope that you will compile your own list in the years ahead.

A list is useless if you cannot get hold of the titles it suggests. The following details are intended to help you to use the Book Lists in a practical way; that is, to get your hands on any particular book that you want to try out with your child.

To begin with, note the details about any book carefully. Title, author and publisher are the most important. If you are not familiar with these terms, examine the title-page at the beginning of this book. The title-page gives the full title, and the names of author, illustrator and publisher. In this case, you will see "Atheneum, New York" at the foot of the title page. The publisher's name or an abbreviation of it also will be found on the spine of the book. Compare the two if you need to check.

On the copyright page, which is usually found on the back of the title page, is the printer's name. This is not important in obtaining a book. Understanding the difference between publisher and printer may help you to avoid confusing them. The publisher creates the book. He either engages an author to write it, or accepts a manuscript already written. In either case, he works with the author to get the book into suitable form for publication. He arranges for illustrations if necessary, designs the layout, and manages all the business details. Then he sends the whole thing to a printer, who uses sophisticated modern machinery to print it. Last of all, it is bound into covers, and delivered to the publishers, who must then distribute it to booksellers and try to make sure that people know of its existence. The printer is no longer involved at this stage.

Let's assume, then, that you have noted the details of a particular title and understand their significance. The next step is to ask at your library, giving all these details. Your librarian will find the requested title by reference to either title or author if the library owns it already, but will be helped by knowing the publisher as well if he decides to obtain it.

You may decide that you want to buy the book, either before or after borrowing it from the library. A well-stocked children's bookshop should have most of the suggested titles in stock, and you may find it more convenient to browse in a bookshop. If the bookshop does *not* have your title in stock and you want to order it, the bookseller will need to know the publisher's name—but a really considerate customer provides all three vital facts: title; author; publisher. A really considerate bookseller, of course, will have catalogues, directories, and perhaps even electronic equipment to help him find elusive titles. Better still, he may have human qualities of imagination, determination and interest.

Some years ago a customer rushed into our bookshop. She had just heard a radio review of "a wonderful new children's book called *Daniel's Garden*" and she wanted to buy it for her small daughter. We had never let her down yet—she knew we would have it ... We gazed blankly at her. Just before her confidence in us, and our pride in our performance ebbed irretrievably away, I found myself saying, "Could you mean—*Joseph's Yard?*" She could! Minutes later she left rejoicing, Charles Keeping's superb latest title clutched to her bosom!

The bookseller may know the title but not have it "in stock" at that moment. In this case, he should be prepared to take your order for it, and advise you when it is available. There is always the possibility that the title is "out of print" and therefore not obtainable, unless you are lucky enough to find a secondhand copy. This is worth trying and can, in most towns and cities, be accomplished by telephone. Most telephone directories list secondhand bookshops in their business sections.

If you have any reason to suspect that the title *is* in print regardless of the bookseller's statement that it is not, you might like to write direct to the publisher. All publishers are deeply interested in the public's attitude to their books, and find it hard to get enough feedback. You never know—your letter may even contribute to a decision to reprint!

Don't hesitate, even if you feel slightly self-conscious, to request details from either librarian or bookseller. Be polite and friendly, but firm. Both exist to give you service. You have a right to the information.

Be sure, also, to include your child in the "finding out" game. He will quickly start using the terms himself: "copy," "title in stock," "out of print." Some years ago I was explaining to my family my inability to procure a particular brand of toothpaste—"Must be out of print," said our five-year-old!

Children feel more sure of themselves, less buffeted by fate and adults, if they are included. They will grow into adults who ask questions, if, as children, they come to expect answers. Bring them up to believe that finding out—about anything—is not only possible, but fun.

Note: After some thought (and experimentation) I have decided to retain the traditional "he" whenever I need a small word to stand for "baby" or "child." I was brought up to believe that the masculine pronoun in these circumstances stood for both girls and boys. If anything, I felt that "she" was rather special. It never had to be shared with boys.

1

Why Books?

From the moment a baby first opens his eyes, he is learning. Sight, sound, and sensation together spark off a learning process which will continue to the end of his life and determine in large measure the sort of person he will become.

Although the process is continuous, however, it is not even. At certain times learning will proceed at almost reckless pace; at others it will seem to have stopped, or at least to be in recess.

Scientists tell us that approximately one half of a person's ultimate intelligence is developed by the age of four, with another thirty per cent accruing by the age of eight. Clearly, what happens during these years matters.

In families where little thought is given to the need for early stimulation, it is quite common for parents to become concerned later about a child's poor progress at school. All too often, this leads to the negative reactions of urging, nagging, blaming ... usually to no avail. The days when the child's whole being radiated a joyful and receptive enthusiasm for learning have passed, unrecognized and little used.

Perhaps this sounds overdramatic. But it is true that the first three or four years are still seen by many people as a time when children are most tiresome, rather than as a period during which learning proceeds at almost breathtaking speed. Toddlers want constantly to touch things which may break, to attempt skills which are beyond them. They ask "why?" and "how?" repetitively and infuriatingly. They shout with rage when thwarted in their destructive purposes and will not learn that this behavior is anti-social and cannot be allowed. These are the constant complaints of some parents. Understandably, they want this stage to pass as quickly as possible.

But take heart! The same period may be seen in another way altogether. How about this?

"Early childhood is a time when children are at their most engaging, when the learning process may be seen with utmost clarity. They want to explore everything, discovering for themselves how things feel, how they work, how they sound when banged together, or dropped. They want to poke knobs and press switches and have a hand in everything. They naturally resent any attempt to curb this interesting experimentation, and protest in the only way they know, with vocally expressed rage."

Which interpretation will *you* have?

I've long believed that a parent's only hope for real living (as against mere survival) during this period is to "opt in"; to become personally involved in the youngster's learning life, so that triumphs and satisfactions, as well as defeats and reversals, feature daily. If you can believe that his latest atrocity is based on a desire to experiment, rather than to torture *you*, you'll feel better. You may be able to devise a harmless game that fulfils the same (apparently diabolical) purpose; but at least your dismay need not be colored by the suspicion that you are raising a monster.

I well remember our consternation when a small son, still under two, discovered that objects could be pried off out-of-reach shelves with a toy spade, an umbrella, a broom. It was bad enough to have one's precious books crashing about; a heavy vase or a potted plant might have killed him. I don't recall any neat solution, but he was not our first child and we managed to avoid the worst excesses of parental outrage. We had learned real humility by the time this child turned into the very constructive and enterprising boy that was lurking beneath the two-year-old horror.

The other outstanding conclusion of scientists that relates to our present purpose is that language stands head and shoulders over all other tools as an instrument of learning. It takes only a little reflection to see that it is language that gives man his lead in intelligence over all other creatures. Only man is capable of abstract thought. Only man can stand off and contemplate his own situation. No other creature can assemble a mental list of ideas, consider them, draw conclusions, and then explain his reasoning. Man can do this because he possesses language; only the most rudimentary thought would be available to him otherwise.

Just a little more reflection produces the conclusion that if thought depends upon language, then the quality of an individual's thought will depend upon the quality of his language. Language is, indeed, in the center of the stage as far as learning and intelligence are concerned.

How *does* a child learn to use language?

From the earliest days, unless he is deaf, a baby will be listening to language. At the same time he will be producing his own sounds, those familiar cooing and gurgling noises, which are characteristic of all human babies. At other times, of course, the noises he produces are strident and angry, making known his hunger, his discomfort, or his need for human contact. But always, from the beginning of life, the sounds the baby produces are an extension of himself. They are his way of expressing his feelings, making his needs known to other human beings. These early noises are, simultaneously, the raw material from which speech will be forged, and the first, instinctive attempt to communicate.

Even as early as a few weeks or a month, a baby will be soothed by a human voice uttering comforting words close to him. This essentially emotional response provides early evidence of a truth that has emerged in the field of language study. Feeling is an important component of language learning. A child learns to use language in interaction with other human beings, and this learning proceeds best against a background of affectionate feedback from the person who is closest to him. This does not have to be his mother, but it does seem that a child's greatest hope of having his language needs totally and joyfully met in his first few years lies in the almost constant presence of one person who loves him, and wants to communicate with him. For it is through such caring, verbal interaction that the child learns best to use language.

At first, his attempt to name an object may be an approximation only. His mother will accept his utterance with pleasure, often repeating it in correct form, or supplying the rest of the sentence which was so clearly implied.

"Ninner!"
"Yes, I know you are hungry and want your dinner."

Long before he utters his first word, however, the child is involved in a two-way process which is steadily and surely building a foundation for his later performance in the language game. Constantly surrounded by language, he is building structures in his mind into which his speech, and later reading, will fit. The form of these structures will depend on the amount and complexity of the speech he hears. The fortunate child in our society listens to articulate adults using language fluently. He will be accustomed to hearing ideas expressed and opinions defended.

He will know, long before he can contribute himself, that relationships are forged through this two-way process of speaking and listening; that warmth and humor have a place in the process, as have all other human emotions.

It seems that language learning has a great deal to do with emotion and the development of relationships. This is seen to perfection in the interaction between parent and baby; eyes locked together, the adult almost physically drawing "verbal" response from the baby, both engulfed by that unique experience of intimate and joyful "connecting" which sets the pattern of relationship between two people.

For the baby, the experience is vital. It has long been believed that the tone of this first relationship carries over into all subsequent relationships, so that the child is equipped (or not) for successful emotional encounters. That language learning also gets its start, for better or worse, during this process, seems clear.

From this point there seems to be a circular process in operation that determines the direction which the child-parent relationship will take. Ideally, the baby's joyful response to the parent's approach sparks off delight and satisfaction in the adult and ensures the continuation of the process. If the adult already uses language fluently, as a major tool of relationship, the baby's language development follows as the night the day. Surely, in every generation since the dawn of civilization, fortunate children and the adults who cared for them have demonstrated this truth.

Why then, do we need to worry about it, or bother describing the process?

Because there is sadly irrefutable evidence that millions of the world's children have no chance at all of finding an adult partner in the early language game. And of these millions, a very large proportion are deprived by ignorance and the circumstances of their lives, rather than the absence of adults who care for them. All too often, language impoverishment is an established fact by the time a child starts school. And language is, undeniably, essential to learning. Tragedy has already entered the life of the five- or six-year-old whose early years have not provided him with the tools of learning.

It must be admitted that the ideas about using books that such a volume as this offers are inaccessible to many of these children and their parents. But this does not mean that these parents are uncaring. In my experience, the vast majority of parents of babies want to do the best they can for their children. Identifying "the best," however, may be difficult, if not impossible.

Persuading such parents to read to their babies is not as unlikely an idea as it may seem at first. It is one that I offer constantly to the young mothers who make up the groups which I am asked to address. These are seldom "educated" young women; more often, they are working-class wives, prey to all the modern ills of loneliness, boredom, strain, and uncertainty that suburban life engenders. One group that stands out in my mind is organized regularly by a psychologist whose work involves contact with a local "drop-in" center for parents. She assures me that these women agree to come to our shop, bringing their babies and toddlers, purely because they so enjoy outings. The fact that this particular outing has as its destination a bookshop may temporarily depress enthusiasm; once arrived, they give every evidence of interest and enjoyment.

We start with coffee and biscuits, and then settle down (in our children's playroom) for the "talk." Informality is the keynote. Babies lie on the mats, or on adult knees, and toddlers play with blocks, dolls and trucks. The mothers have been advised to bring provisions for the children, so bottles, diapers and teddy bears are in evidence. The mothers' initial apprehension about their children's behavior soon evaporates . . . as I am sitting on a low stool and using delectable picture books for demonstration, I am soon surrounded by an attentive audience—and there is always a wide-eyes baby to borrow, for proof of my assertion that babies will attend to picture and print!

It is difficult to persuade parents to read to nine-year-olds, or even six-year-olds, if the practice has not been established early. The children may resist, suspecting the adult's motive, or be unprepared to believe that the experience will be enjoyable. Many adults are keenly aware of their own shortcomings in the reading-aloud field. But babies are quite uncritical, and utterly accepting of adult attention; they provide a totally captive audience, accomplishing marvels in parental self-esteem. And practice does make perfect. The assured adult presenter of *Harry the Dirty Dog*, three years later, will have quite forgotten his fumbling performance on *B is for Bear*, all those years ago!

It is my firm belief that giving the parent the idea of "the book as a tool" will do more for the dual purpose of establishing the parent-child relationship and insuring the child's adequate language development, than any amount of advice on *talking* to babies. None of us can endlessly initiate speech; we run out of ideas, or just plain get sick of it. The lives of babies and toddlers, even favored ones, are limited. The experience just isn't there to provide the raw material for constant verbal interaction without inevitable bordeom on the child's part and desperation on the adult's. But if books are added . . .

It is not possible to gauge the width and depth of the increase in a child's grasp of the world that comes with access to books. Contact with children of very tender years—two and three years of age—engenders a sense of awe at the way their understanding outruns their capacity for expression, the way their speech strains constantly to encompass their awareness, to represent reality as they see it. Shades of meaning, which may be quite unavailable to the child of limited language experience, are startlingly present in the understanding—and increasingly in the speech—of the "well-read-to" toddler.

A small grandson, nearly twenty-three months old, preceded me up the stairs yesterday. Straining to hold the handrail, which he could hardly reach, he stumbled and recovered himself.

"Nearly fell," he said. Then fearing that perhaps this failed to cover the situation exactly, he added "Almost!" This little boy looks like a two-year-old and certainly exhibits the full range of two-year-old characteristics (by turn, engaging and enraging). But his range of reference, his appreciation of degree, and in particular his consciousness of language and the way it *works* is impressive.

He lives with his parents in a very isolated area, several hundred miles away. When they arrived on holiday recently, he spoke beautifully, saying, "yes," whenever the affirmative was called for. Under the influence of the adolescents in the family, he converted "yes" to "yeah" in no time at all. At dinner one night someone mentioned this. Our two-year-old gave every sign of appreciating the difference and its significance. "Not yess-ss!" he shouted, banging his spoon and laughing. "Yeah!" He seemed to understand the general merriment in an uncannily mature way. Earlier he had corrected his mother when she referred by name to a character encountered for the first time in a new book this morning. "Doctor *Crank,*" he said firmly, in response to her tentative "Doctor Shanks?" Earlier still, in a department store he had been whisked without preparation on to an escalator, a totally new experience. His dismay was fast turning to panic by the time his mother's reassurance came. "Remember? Corduroy went on an escalator." One could almost see his reinterpretation of the experience as familiar. If his good friend Corduroy could go on an escalator, so could Anthony!

In this family, mother and small son spend many hours alone together, in near-blizzard conditions for much of the year. Anthony's father is often away until the little boy is in bed, and company is difficult to provide. His mother's way of filling the long hours has always involved books. He has been read to constantly, as much for his parents' needs as his own, from birth.

At nearly two, he is the most "experienced" toddler I know—and yet a huge proportion of this experience has been at second hand. His first visit to the zoo was a journey for redis-covery. "Zebra!" "Giraffe!" "Lion!" Let no "expert" persuade you that the small child should be introduced, in books, only to those objects that he has experienced in the flesh. Anthony has made joyful acquaintance with countless people, animals, objects and ideas, all between the covers of books, in his first two years of life, to his own incalculable advantage.

To strike one last, I hope conclusive blow for the introduc-tion of books to preschoolers, let me establish the connection be-tween early book usage and later skills in reading.

It is useless to deny that there is, here and there, a child who will have difficulty in learning to read despite having been sur-rounded by books from an early age. This child probably has some specific learning difficulty, which may be impossible to diagnose except in the most general way. But he does have some rare but *real* disability.

For every such child, there are thousands whose reading fail-ure seems unrelated to any specific handicap. They just can't read, at an age by which reading has usually been mastered. These are the children who are, almost inevitably, "short" on language; short on concepts, on the "pattterns" of the tongue of their culture. Book language is an unfathomable mystery to them. It is a foreign language, not their own. I believe that these chil-dren need, more than anything else, a crash course in listening; to people who have something to say to them, and want to hear their ideas in return; to stories that will expand their view of the world; stories that will stir their emotions and quicken their curiosity. Then there may be some chance of these children reading for themselves—if caring, good-humored people will only guide them through the mechanics and show them that most of what they need for reading they have already, in their own minds, and bodies, and hearts.

There is nothing magic about the way contact with books in early years produces early readers. One would surely expect it to.

A baby is learning about the way language arises from the page each time his parent opens a book, from earliest days. He is linking the human voice to the print at a very early age. Given repeated opportunity, he notices how the adult attends to the black marks, how he can't go on reading if the page is turned too soon . . .

Skills come apparently unbidden as the toddler advances into three- and four-year-old independence. Print is friendly and familiar for this child. He is already unconsciously finding landmarks, noting regular features, predicting patterns . . .

Unbidden? Not a bit of it! This child has had his reading skills handed him on a golden platter.

2

Too Little to Look?

I am the sister of him
And he is my brother,
But he is too little for us to
Talk to each other;
So every morning I show him
My doll and my book,
But every morning he still is
Too little to look.

Ideally, a small pile of good books awaits the new baby's arrival. Friends and relations often request suggestions for presents, and gift money can be earmarked for books. In my family, we have a habit of sending a book for the "displaced" baby. *Mr Grumpy's Outing*, "For Jane, and Timothy, when he is old enough," is of much more use in a delicate family situation than a pair of bootees!

Keep the baby's books within reach, and make a practice of

showing them to him from the day you first bring him home. The covers will be brightly illustrated, and at first you can encourage him to focus his eyes on these pictures. You can teach your baby a lot about books in the first few months.

To begin with, he will learn that a book is a thing, with different qualities from all other things. For many babies, the world must flow past in a succession of half-perceived images. Until their own physical development enables them to lift and turn their heads and focus their eyes, they must rely on obliging adults to help.

As early in his life as possible, start showing your baby successive pages of a suitable book. If you don't believe that this is making a start on his learning life, at least you'll believe that for both of you, it is an agreeable way of spending time. Babies love to be held, and you will be getting your hand in early.

You will need books which have clearly defined, uncluttered pictures, in bright primary colors. The work of a Dutchman, Dick Bruna, is worth knowing about. Bruna books are simplicity itself. An apple, in *b is for bear*, is a bright red sphere, slightly indented where a green stalk is attached. The whole is outlined in black on a white page. I have yet to meet a very young baby who is not arrested by Bruna's apple.

Give him time to soak it up, meanwhile pointing to the black "a" on the opposite page and saying anything that comes to mind; "A is for apple" to start with, then any other cheerful and relevant comment. "Look at the big, red apple." Don't worry, when you come to successive pages, that he may never see a real live Eskimo or that castles are remote from his experience; "E is for Eskimo" and "C for castle" will be accepted in good faith, and their representations savored. Other "first" Brunas are listed in the relevant section at the end of the chapter. Not all titles are suitable for the earliest listener, and the standard varies considerably.

Most of the books suggested in this chapter have been written for young children rather than babies. Even in the world of book production, the notion that babies need books is slow to take root. But why worry if the characters in his books are operating at a level the baby will not reach for several years? This is true of the people around him, who walk, talk, and conduct their lives in complex ways before his sponge-like contemplation. How much could he possibly learn from the boring company of other babies?

Babies need people: talking, laughing, warm-hearted people, constantly drawing them into their lives, and offering them the world for a playground. Let's give them books to parallel this experience; books where language and illustration activate the senses, so that meaning slips in smoothly, in the wake of feeling.

Alphabet books seem to be particularly useful at this stage, probably because so many of them are very simple. Brian Wildsmith's *ABC* is a feast of rich color, a delight for any age. It has become, deservedly, a modern classic. John Burningham's *ABC* will be favored by some parents, and is loved in my own family. Burningham's king and queen are masterly and majestic; and the sooner babies start making the acquaintance of the monarchs of fiction, in word and in picture, the better. There is a spirited pair in Rodney Peppé's *The Alphabet Book*. Each double spread in this excellent ABC covers two successive letters; a single line of simple text at the bottom of the page accentuates the appropriate letter, which is both larger and more heavily printed than the others.

This is the **a**nchor . . . that holds the **b**oat.
Here is a **C**upboard. Count the **d**olls.

(which are revealed sitting in three engaging rows, once the cupboard is opened)

Start *now*, running your finger casually under the text as you say it. Not always, but occasionally. By the time your baby is old enough to connect the black marks on the page with your voice, the knowledge that the meaning arises from the writing will have lodged in his bones. Peppé's illustrations are particularly suited to the very young child's need for clarity, color, and no-clutter. *The Alphabet Book* is a totally satisfying experience, with its square, stiffish pages, and striking pictures.

Helen Oxenbury's ABC of Things, a tall, narrow book which offers a number of "things" connected in cheerful, non-sensical fashion, is transformed by this artists' unique and hu-morous drawings into a masterpiece. Her *Number of Things* is equally satisfying.

"Number" and "color" books seem made for the under-ones, too, and remember that these, like alphabet books, all come into their own again once the child is learning to read, to count, and to recognize colors.

One to Eleven by a Japanese artist, Yutaka Sugita, is an out-standing book; a wonderful present for a one-year-old (and his parents), and a thing of beauty. This is a volume that adults may be tempted to preserve from little hands while exposing it to ap-preciative eyes. Each wide double spread, a celebration of bril-liant color and exciting form, almost asks to be framed and hung!

Jan Piénkowski as an artist has many moods, but nowhere has he more clearly met a real need than in a set of small, square volumes entitled *Colors, Sizes, Numbers* and *Shapes*. The first two of these are probably the most useful, though all arrest the baby's eye with that same brilliance and clarity that characterizes Bruna's work. Their size (17 cm × 17 cm) is important too; for attention-getting, a small, easily manipulated book is best.

There is another useful category, which my family calls "noise" books. These are loved by very small children, not least because they demand adult performance. In *A Noisy Book* by Ross Thomson, for example, a succession of vigorous activities is depicted in bold outline, and the appropriate noise is represented by strident crazy letters sprawling across the pages.

Trouble in the Ark, by Gerald Rose, though ostensibly an

early reader, is also an excellent noise book. It begins with the animals crowded together in the ark. A fly starts the trouble; "he *buzzed* at mouse, who *squeaked* at rabbit, who *squealed* at rhinoceros ..." Inevitably, hen cackles, wolf howls, lion roars ... until "just then, dove flew in with an olive twig," at which stage Noah himself adds to the rumpus with a sustained "Yahoo! Yippee!" which can be relied upon to delight the young, accompanied as it inevitably will be with wild bouncing-on-parental-knee! Here is language that is rich, action that is headlong, and humor that is compelling. Vigorous, clear and colorful pictures of each animal annoying his neighbor render the whole a joy.

Peter Spier has produced several "noise" books, each astonishingly comprehensive in its field. I remember emerging from a prolonged and inforced performance of *Gobble, Growl, Grunt* with racked vocal chords and ruined throat while on holiday with several grandchildren some years ago. The tyrant of the piece was a grandson of two-and-a-half whose enthusiasm for this book knew no bounds. His sister, aged six, disapproved strongly of it. "It's not a real story at all," she declared firmly, and I agreed. But I was no match for her brother! No one else offered to perform, and I weakly continued. (The children's parents pointed out with some justification that I had given it to him for Christmas. They also contrived to leave it behind when they left a few days before we did!)

"Noise" books are almost, but not quite, gimmicky; but they are fun, and may be used with babies long before their point is understood. A similar purpose is served by so-called "manipulative" books, which inevitably invite page-turning-plus. In *Little, Big, Bigger* by Beth Clure and Helen Rumsey, the stiff, easily-turned pages are of varying widths. Successive turning reveals "a little dog   a big dog   a bigger dog ... a little car   a big car   a bigger car." The book is hugely successful with babies; its color is brilliant, its text brief to the point of terseness (it is of course, a theme book as well). The one- to two-year-old will love the success he can experience by flipping over the page and altering the size of the dog, house, car. *Where is Home?*, by the same authors and artist, is a "flap" book. Each right-hand page is folded in such a way that part of the picture is hidden. Each left-hand page asks a question: "Where is home for the baby chicks?" The answer is revealed when the flap is opened, a skill that is easy to master in this book, where the pages are stiff and smooth.

H. A. Rey produced a set of flap books in the 1950s and these, despite a tendency to triteness, have more than proved the popularity of this device with the young. *Where's My Baby?*, which confines its text to a rhyming four-line stanza on each left-hand page, is suitable for first-year use; the other titles have text and rather more complicated themes, and will come into their own a year or so later.

This is probably the place to insert a few hints about the physical management of read-aloud sessions.

The baby is, of course, totally captive only while he is still unable to use his arms and hands for batting and snatching. Thereafter, you will have to find some course that is acceptable to both of you; that will neither totally frustrate him, nor so thwart *your* purpose that you give up.

To begin with, you must accept that any baby worth his salt *will* want to grab the book as soon as his physical development renders this possible. This does not mean that he is not interested; on the contrary, he is *so* interested that he wants to experience that delectable object (the book) in the way he likes best of all. He wants to grab it and cram it into his mouth! (If you find this kind of reaction too exasperating, try to imagine what it's like to be a parent whose baby, for some tragic reason, cannot use his hands to grab anything).

Your best course of action is to play for time. If you can arrange for him to experience real visual and aural satisfaction from contact with book, you may find that he modifies his snatching behavior at a surprisingly early age. Be sure to give him a rattle or similar toy to suck while listening and watching, and remember that, even at this early stage, a dramatic performance, with actions and changes of voice tone, will be more entertaining than a monotonous one.

For your own sake, read aloud an interesting, lively story from time to time. Endless improvisation on the near-textless page can be tiring and boring. One of my daughters read *The Elephant and the Bad Baby* which is, strictly speaking, suitable for older children, to her small son, frequently, from five months, as this book was available and she enjoyed it herself. Shortly afterwards, *The Very Hungry Caterpillar*, *Whistle for Willie*, and *The Little Fire Engine* were introduced for the same reason, with *Harquin* following shortly after. This young mother mentioned a point that hadn't occurred to me in this connection; it is possible to feel quite self-conscious, carrying on an endless one-way conversation with a very young baby, whereas reading aloud is a *performance!*

And to this performance, as to any other, you can bring spirit and individuality. Don't hesitate to move in time to the rhythm, to accentuate rhymes, to tickle or cuddle the baby at appropriate points (which he will come to anticipate), to turn over the page with a flourish . . . in short, to perform with style.

Your reward will come with your baby's response. You'll be astonished at how early he gives sign of knowing that, any minute now, the image will change. As your hand moves towards the top right-hand corner of the page, the baby's eyes will brighten. A flick—and a totally new vista is presented for his delight. You are staying in touch with him in the best possible way, if you can share his pleasure.

And please—please!—don't give up because your baby snatches at the book and appears to want only to eat it or throw it away. Cancelling the whole program in the face of a few setbacks is like deciding to keep your child well away from the water until he can swim! There is ample evidence that three- and four-year-olds who meet books for the first time in their lives are inattentive and destructive. Your baby can put this stage behind him in his very early days, if you are patient. A little and often, is the rule of thumb!

You may wonder why I have not mentioned either rag, or board books earlier. Many people assume that these are true "baby" books: that the "real" variety enter children's lives only when they are old enough to understand their value, and handle them carefully.

About rag books, let me say only that I do not consider them to be books. Books are made of paper, which, in all its various forms, nonetheless looks, feels, smells, sounds, and *behaves* like paper. Rag books look, feel, sound and behave like limp dishrags, and before long, smell like *dirty* limp dishrags. I deplore them and am comforted only by the conviction that babies will not be deluded into thinking they *are* books.

A placticized material which looks reasonably like paper and yet will not tear has been used by several mass market producers to make books for babies. So far, color and content have been indifferent; but the idea is a useful one, and the species may improve. The material is certainly an advance on cloth; but still, not paper. (I am an incurable purist, I admit.)

Board books pose different problems. I can accept them—uneasily—as books, while doubting the need for their existence. As their only possible justification must be that babies can safely handle them alone, there is no point in supplying text. Indeed, *The Christmas Story* by Hilde Heyduck-Huth, a Nativity celebration of simple but breathtaking beauty, is frustrated in its true purpose by its "board" nature. One cannot find it in most libraries, and schools consider, quite rightly, that their pupils need real books. By its format then, this superb title, in which picture and text complement one another harmoniously, is denied access to its proper audience.

Bodley Head has produced a series which I suggest you inspect if you feel that your baby would take pleasure in a board book. These attractive little volumes see their role honestly; the flexible pages avoid the heavy, unyielding quality of the conventional cardboard type, and can be sponged without marking. Clear and colorful pictures of everyday objects are shown against uncluttered backgrounds. No text, thank goodness. The three animal titles are possibly the most appealing, with *Farm Animals* by Betty Youngs taking my vote as the most engaging board book in the field. How can one resist a donkey engineered in purple lace? And surely, cows were meant to have corduroy hides?

A common mistake on the part of new parents is the assumption that for young children photographs of objects and scenes are preferable to drawings, paintings, or other art forms. This is seldom true.

Have you ever wondered why botany textbooks—or seamen's manuals—use *drawings* of plants and ships rather than photographs to illustrate their points? This is because an artist can include the features he needs for his purpose, and just as importantly, exclude those features which would distract the human eye, or mar the clarity of the intended impression. It is essential, in a serious textbook, that the shape, outline and detail of the represented object be shown in a way that permits no mistake. Thus, the author arranges for drawings, not photographs, to illustrate his points.

If students and adults find pictures simpler to follow than photographs, surely one would expect the young child to show similar preference? The three-dimensional quality of a photograph is a complication to a small child. There is a feeling abroad that it is important that small children recognize and name objects in their books. Even in this connection, flat representations win out.

And now to nursery rhymes.

Don't even consider facing parenthood without a really good collection. We all think we can remember them, but how many can we call to mind, offhand? Modern teachers tell us that many children come to school without knowing any.

You may ask, "Of what value are nursery rhymes in today's world?"

To begin with, nursery rhymes are part of our children's heritage, in an age when too little is handed down. There is a world of security and satisfaction in knowing that children don't really change from generation to generation; that some of the best things are still the oldest. We feel part of a great human progression as we see our children swept into the dance as we were before them. We convey our own deep satisfaction in this process, and rejoice in our children's in return.

And the rhymes themselves? Many of them began as political jingles concocted by adults, but over the years the children have taken them for their own. They have been polished and shined and their corners smoothed, until their form is, in many cases, perfect. If children are to have poetry later, they need to discover early the peculiar satisfaction that comes from experiencing form in language. This is not something that can ever be taught; how can a sensation be taught? But it will be there, in their repertoire of response, if it has been kindled in babyhood.

You may have to take this assertion on trust, if poetry has meant little to you in your own life. You may even doubt that it matters anyway, and this doubt is understandable. Fortunately, you can relax, and use nursery rhymes and other poems with your baby without examining their long term effects at all. The evidence will be undeniable that the baby loves them *now*. They are a real aid when you and your child are obliged to make the best of one another's company (as when you are driving and he is strapped into his car seat) or when you find yourself temporarily stranded without a book. You will certainly notice the way the rhymes bubble out of him once they are entrenched. You can hear the way his flow of language is improved with this constant repetition, see the way he moves joyfully to the rhythm, sense the satisfaction he feels in the rhyme. Patterns are being laid down here; patterns into which every sort of later literary and musical experience will fit.

You may still feel that some of the nursery rhymes are too nonsensical for modern use. In this workaday world, shouldn't our children be hearing only good sense?

Not a bit of it! An element of lunacy has always been cherished by children, and words that are not completely rational, but that offer an experience to the senses rather than the mind, help them towards a feeling for language itself, in all its diverse trappings. We are surely hoping to raise imaginative children, children who tap all the available resources, without and within? At all events, overseriousness had no place in childhood.

The nursery rhyme edition you choose matters less than your own willingness to perform. It is better to have no book at all, if you are confident about your off-the-cuff talent, than to invest in an expensive volume and leave it on the shelf. The essential factor is your determination to surround your child with the jingles and rhymes of his culture; to invite his response to rhythm and rhyme, to gladden his heart and enliven his imagination.

The Mother Goose Treasury by Raymond Briggs is unlikely to be surpassed as a comprehensive popular collection. The illustrations achieve a superb compromise between the "traditional" (which is usually Victorian) and the modern, and have a clarity and robust vigor, which appeal to child and adult alike. You may prefer the meticulous dignity and quiet color of Kathleen Lines's *Lavender's Blue,* or the lavish purples and scarlets of Brian Wildsmith's *Mother Goose.* Your baby won't protest, so you may as well buy with your own pleasure in mind. You'll be more likely to use the book if you love it, and this is what matters. It may even seem (and be) good sense to start with a cheap, mass market version, or a paperback, while you make up your mind— or until Grandma resolves the matter by producing one that you hadn't encountered in your browsing.

I have heard a parent say, when shown one of the big collections of nursery rhymes, "It seems such a big book for such a little child," and I understand this feeling. Briggs's *Treasury* certainly has to be supported by table, floor, or bed while being read, and a small child could hardly carry it safely.

Ideally, the collection of one's choice should be kept on table or shelf, and produced for shared sessions until the child is old enough to handle the book alone. You need not feel that these supervised sessions are repressive if the toddler has several small, cheap editions of his own—perhaps Hilda Boswell's *Treasury of Nursery Rhymes* in paperback, and one or two of the Ladybird series.

Perfect for holding in one hand and reading aloud is *Nicola Bayley's Book of Nursery Rhymes*, but its indescribable beauty may make you reluctant to risk impetuous little fingers! This book has the air of a collection of prints; I have yet to meet an adult who is not simultaneously astonished and enchanted by it. A wonderful present for a new family!

Barry Wilkinson's illustrations for *Sally Go Round the Sun* evoke Raymond Briggs in their spirit and brilliance, and yet are thoroughly individual. The forty-six nursery rhymes in this collection occur one to a page throughout the book, and have been very well chosen for the youngest child; here are assembled the basic, essential rhymes. This book's size (17 cm × 21 cm) is ideal, I suspect, for holding and showing to a baby or small child. Larger pages are inclined to crumple as they are turned, and a human hand cannot hold a heavier, larger book rigid for any length of time without strain.

The same dimensions are shared by an outstanding picture book, *Humpty Dumpty and Other First Rhymes*, illustrated by Betty Youngs, of *Farm Animals* board book fame. This book demonstrates the absolute luxury of one rhyme to one opening; undeniably the best arrangement for the very young. These are collage pictures of infinite ingenuity and detail. They have texture, miraculously evoked, and incredible variety. The patchwork-quilt endpapers invite the hand to stroke, the mind to linger.

I would start with shared perusal of this wonder, read the title-page aloud as part of the book (it is too good to miss), and enjoy the second set of endpapers, before closing it. Only the editor's willingness to confine its text to eight rhymes allows this double-spread treatment, and it was an inspired decision. This is not a collection; it is a picture book to be read in entirety, dwelt upon, and savored.

Several illustrators have chosen only those rhymes that involve particular animals, and have, in their ingenuity, conjured up a variety of little-known, as well as familiar rhymes.

Rodney Peppé's *Cat and Mouse* has a graphic balance that rivets the adult as well as the child eye to the page. The size and shape (21 cm wide × 19 cm deep) is again, pleasing and manageable, and the shiny black cover, with engagingly predatory pussy devouring (with eyes alone) a fat little mouse who is saying "eek!", irresistible.

Hark! Hark! the Dogs do Bark, *This Little Pig-a-Wig* and *Mittens for Kittens* by Erik and Lenore Blegvad, while less arresting in their presentation than *Cat and Mouse*, have a quiet appeal that springs from their choice of rhymes and the aptness of the small, neat but expressive illustrations. Small in format, and not too long to read at a sitting, these are satisfying, eloquent little books.

A natural extension of the nursery rhyme collection is the song book, complete with music. If you can play the piano, and have one in your home, your children will be especially lucky; but supplying such a book is a good idea, anyway. Most of us are familiar with the tunes for "Jack and Jill," "Three Blind Mice" and "The Farmer in the Dell" and learning that the little black dots and handles on the five-barred fence tell your voice where to go will do the baby no harm. You will almost certainly have a relation or friend who can demonstrate—perhaps on a guitar or recorder if no piano is available—with subsequent increase of interest in this different and fascinating book.

Several very comprehensive collections are available and most of them are, for good measure, well-produced and attractive. *The Baby's Song Book* by Elizabeth Poston contains more than eighty nursery rhymes, with simple piano accompaniment, and is perhaps best of all to begin with. William Stobbs's brilliantly colored pictures adorn each page, and the book itself is accommodating; it sits well on the piano, and lies flat when open on a table.

Songs, of course, are for any and all age groups, as long as they are lyrical and uncomplicated. *The Great Song Book* by Timothy John ranges from nursery rhymes through folk songs to lullabies and carols and has an extra bonus in its addition of guitar chords to the simple settings. This is a whole-of-life book for a family to grow on. Tomi Ungerer's superbly set illustrations and the sturdy, manageable nature of the book itself make *The Great Song Book* an especially valuable possession. Persuading a fond grandparent to provide it as a first birthday present is worth thinking about!

This may be a good time to state a belief I hold about duplication in books for the young. Far from rejecting a rhyme or poetry book (or later, a story collection) because it contains material available in already-owned titles, try to make sure that this repetition does occur. The child whose own familiar Humpty Dumpty resides between the covers of Brigg's *Treasury* will greet his prototype in other collections with cries of joyful recognition. This is an essentially human reaction; we all have it. If the version is slightly different read it as presented. The sooner small children become interested in the fascinating tendency of rhyme and story to vary from time to time and place to place, the better. Of course no one parent could afford to buy five or six editions to facilitate this process, but perhaps the major family collection of nursery rhymes could be augmented—and given new life—by one of those shorter gems? If you add library borrowing, reciprocal arrangements with friends and the odd paperback, you could raise a connoisseur!

One last word. My own favorite collection was published in 1958, looks like a real book, not a picture book, and is labelled simply *Nursery Rhymes, Collected and Illustrated by A. H. Watson.* Each of its rhymes is supported by scrupulously accurate little line drawings. Sameness is avoided by the use, on successive pages, of different colored inks for the illustrations: black, red, brown, blue, orange. Like all titles in The Children's Illustrated Classics series, this book is beautifully bound and faultlessly produced. A book for a grandparent to own, perhaps, and for visiting grandchildren to learn to love. Its difference from the better-known, more colorful Mother Goose collections is one of its greatest charms.

It is hard to draw the line between nursery rhymes and what I call "jingles." Where, in your classification, do "This little Pig went to Market . . ." and "Frère Jacques . . ." belong? No need to decide. Several thoroughly competent editors have taken the matter into their own hands and provided staple editions, which ensure that the field is covered.

This Little Puffin, compiled by Elizabeth Matterson, should be provided as a matter of course. Its low price is fortunate, as you will certainly wear out several copies. It describes itself as "a remarkable treasury of finger plays and singing and action games . . ." and goes on to prove this claim incontestably.

Ladybird has given the field six irreproachable little volumes entitled severally *Action, Dancing, Finger, Memory, Number* and *Talking Rhymes*. If any rhyme worth using has been omitted from this series, I have yet to notice it; and the obvious advantage of being able to collect these six splendid little books at no great expense, one at a time, is considerable. A selection from the series, called *The Ladybird Book of Rhymes*, makes a very good present, and, for its size and presentation, is very good value. But the six little books are my choice.

Some years ago, I advanced upon the hospital in which my first grandchild had just been born bearing a copy of Norah Montgomerie's *This Little Pig Went to Market*. My husband at my side, bore a great armload of summer flowers for our first daughter and her brand-new daughter, but I think that *This Little Pig* probably had greater impact on their lives. Subtitled *Play Rhymes for Infants and Young Children*, this collection is still my favorite among the jingle books. You will have to decide whether sentimentality has overtaken critical faculty here. But few artists draw children who live and breathe as well as Margery Gill. And don't parents' needs matter, as well as children's?

Each of the books I have mentioned is a "how to" book; that is, it tells you not only which rhymes and jingles to use with your baby, but, in detail, how to handle him, tickle, pat, rock and jog him, enlivening the performance with the words. The jingle is the pudding and the actions are the sauce, or vice versa . . .

You will find that you sing some of the rhymes, always, and say others. Respond in your own individual way to jingles; follow the suggestions given for actions if you wish, or invent your own. Before long, rhymes will come unbidden, to accompany the mundane round of life. Your baby's days will be enriched, and your task lightened.

Human response to touch and sound gets its start here. Too many of our children grow up lacking the capacity to use *all* their senses, physical, emotional and intellectual. "It is the world's one crime its babes grow dull . . ." said the poet Vachel Lindsay nearly fifty years ago. We have done little to negate this charge since then.

Make sure that both you and your child emerge from the years of babyhood with all the old rhymes tucked safely away, as familiar as diapers and teddy bears, and just as essential. You will both be well armed for the years ahead.

BOOK LIST 1

Books to Use in the First Year

The titles listed here are suitable for introduction in the first year of a baby's life, but will be in use for years. For ease of reference, titles have been grouped in categories.

Those titles that are mentioned in the previous chapter are marked with a bullet (●). The name of the hardback publisher is given first in the brackets, followed by that of the paperback publisher, where there is one. Those not available in America are marked (GB).

Please use this list in conjunction with the one at the end of the next chapter. There is a great deal of overlap between all the lists.

ALPHABET BOOKS

● (GB) *ABC*   John Burningham   (Cape)

● (GB) *ABC*   Brian Wildsmith   (Watts)

abc   Gerald Witcomb   (Ladybird)
A rather ordinary but useful little book. Ladybird books are so inexpensive that you may decide to let the baby cut his teeth on one, literally! Everyday objects (an apple, a jug, an umbrella) help the baby to see the way in which books represent the world.

● (GB) *The Alphabet Book*   Rodney Peppé   (Kestral)

● (GB) *b Is for Bear*   Dick Bruna   (Methuen)

● (GB) *Helen Oxenbury's ABC of Things*   Helen Oxenbury   (Heinemann)

NUMBER AND COUNTING BOOKS

I can count   Dick Bruna   (Methuen)
Brilliant slabs of primary color in the tradition established by *b is*

for bear. Small, comfortable format makes this, with the next title, a real first book.

● *Numbers* Jan Pieńkowski (Harvey)

● *Numbers of Things* Helen Oxenbury (Watts)

● *Goodnight, One, Two, Three* Yutaka Sugita (Scroll)

(Note: Several titles with counting themes as listed under JINGLES etc.)

NOISE BOOKS

● *Gobble, Growl, Grunt* Peter Spier (Doubleday)

● *A Noisy Book* Ross Thomson (Scroll Pr.)

● (GB) *Trouble in the Ark* Gerald Rose (Faber/Puffin paperback)

MANIPULATIVE BOOKS

● (GB) *Little, Big, Bigger*

● (GB) *Where Is Home?* both by Beth Clure and Helen Rumsey, illus. Jacques Rupp (Bowmar-Noble)

● *Where's My Baby?* H. A. Rey (Houghton-Mifflin)

BOARD BOOKS

● *Farm Animals* Betty Youngs (Bodley Head)

Animals Babies and *Toys* by Robert Broomfield, *Indoors* and *Out-of-doors* by Maureen Roffey, and *Wild Animals* by William Stobbs are other titles I would use with babies from the (Chatto Bodley Jonathan) board book series. All are bright, clear and uncluttered—and almost indestructible.

In the Village H. Heyduck-Huth (Harcourt Brace Jovanovich)

This is the brightest and best (for babies) of eight remarkably beautiful, well-made board books.

NURSERY RHYMES AND OTHER VERSE

● (GB) *Cat and Mouse*   Rodney Peppé   (Kestrel)

(GB) *A First Ladybird Book of Nursery Rhymes*   Frank Hampson   (Ladybird)

(GB) *A Second Ladybird Book of Nursery Rhymes*   Frank Hampson   (Ladybird)

(GB) *A Third Ladybird Book of Nursery Rhymes*   Frank Hampson   (Ladybird)
Three modest little volumes, one rhyme to a page, to keep as "extras" for handbag or car.

(GB) *The Great Big Book of Nursery Rhymes*   Peggy Blakely, illus. Frank Francis   (A. & C. Black)
This sturdy volume has ninety-two rhymes, most of which are drawn from titles in this publisher's Fact and Fancy series. Each left-hand page has one rhyme printed in clear, large letters. Opposite, the whole page is devoted to a vigorous, uncluttered and yet expressive illustration in bright, bold color. This is an exuberant, hearty collection with some enchanting, less well-known rhymes as well as the usual assemblage. The shorter titles have the same landscape format, and are just as attractive. They are: *Bangalorey Man; Silver Nutmeg; Golden Pear; Jack-a-Dandy; Silver Buckles; Three Little Ghostesses;* and *Red Herrings*.

● *Hark! Hark! The Dogs Do Bark*

● *Mittens for Kittens*

● *This Little Pig-a-Wig* all by Erik and Lenore Blegvad   (Atheneum)

● (GB) *Humpty Dumpty and Other First Rhymes*   Betty Youngs   (Bodley Head)

● *Lavender's Blue* Kathleen Lines, illus. Harold Jones (Oxford)

● *Mother Goose* Brian Wildsmith (Watts)

● *The Mother Goose Treasury* Raymond Briggs (Coward)

● *Nicola Bayley's Book of Nursery Rhymes* Nicola Bayley (Knopf)

● *Nursery Rhymes* A. H. Watson (Dent, Biblio Dist.)

The Owl and the Pussycat Edward Lear, illus. Gwen Fulton (Atheneum)
"The sooner the better" is the rule for introducing children to Edward Lear's incomparable nonsense rhymes and this handy little version of the most famous rhyme is just right for babies. They need never recall a time when they didn't know it!

● (GB) *Sally Go Round the Sun* David Mackay, Brian Thompson and Pamela Schaub, illus. Barry Wilkinson (Kestrel/Longman paperback)

The Tall Book of Mother Goose Feodor Rojankorsky (Harper & Row, New York)
An established classic, this title owes part of its success to its unusually tall, narrow shape. The pages have a satisfying robustness, the friendly, colorful illustrations well balanced by the large, clear text.

● *Treasury of Nursery Rhymes* Hilda Boswell (Collins)
A pleasant collection, with conventional but colorful illustrations. The paperback version is handy to keep in the car or handbag for emergency use.

SONG BOOKS

● The Children's Song Book Elizabeth Poston, illus. Susan Einzig (Chatto Bodley Jonathon)

(GB) *The Faber Book of Nursery Songs* D. Mitchell & C. Blyton, illus. Alan Howard (Faber)
A sturdy, established collection of simple songs in simple settings. Black-and-white illustrations (on most pages) are spirited and the colored, whole-page pictures a delight.

● *The Great Song Book* Timothy John, illus. Tomi Ungerer (Doubleday)

JINGLES, ACTION RHYMES AND FINGER PLAYS

● (GB) *Action Rhymes, Dancing Rhymes, Finger Rhymes, Memory Rhymes, Number Rhymes, Talking Rhymes*, all by Dorothy Taylor (Ladybird)

(GB) *One Two Three Four* ed. Mary Grice, illus. Denis Wrigley (Warne)
A very useful collection of rhymes and finger plays, linked by their "counting" theme. The large, clear print ensures a long life for this title; children learning to read will rediscover it several years later. Agreeable, clear line illustrations.

● (GB) *This Little Pig Went to Market* Norah Montgomerie, illus. Margery Gill (Bodley Head)

● (GB) *This Little Puffin* Elizabeth Matterson (Puffin paperback)

INDIVIDUAL TITLES

Hush Little Baby Aliki (Prentice-Hall, New Jersey)
This gentle old lullaby, here seen in an American pioneering setting, is a memorable experience. Deep and sombre browns, oranges and yellows are in tune with the sleepy nature of the song. There is much to be said for acquiring this picture book in the first year. The lullaby will be committed to memory, and the book itself loved for a long time.

(GB) *I See a Lot of Things*   Dean Hay   (Collins)
Beautifully produced photographs of simple objects (a brush and comb, a ball, a teddy bear) with large, clear labels beneath. Like the Ladybird *abc*, this book will help a baby to learn that real things occur in books, and give practice identifying them.

(GB) *The Jumping Up and Down Book*   Jonathon Coudrille   (Whizzard-Deutsch)
A most unusually presented book, combining a jaunty, nonsensical rhyming text and simple but striking illustrations. This is almost a noise book; it calls for vigorous performance. Different kinds of dances are suggested:

> Hopping like a frog dance Plonk! Plonk! Plonk!
> Walking like a robot Clonk, Clonk, Clonk.

The noise words are printed in bright red, and in some cases strewn about the page. A rollicking experience!

My Teddy Bear   Chiyoko Nakatani   (T. Y. Crowell)
Simple text and clear, colorful pictures gently reflect a small child's love for his "best friend."

(GB) *Teddy's Toys*   Grete Janus Hertz, illus. Iben Claute   (Methuen)
"Here is Teddy" announces the first page of this excellent miniature book. "And here are his toys, all stuck in a box. What's Teddy got?" asks the second. Subsequent pages supply the answers in picture and simple text. Bright primary colors ensure attention.

3

When I Was One ...
I had just begun.

In the second year of life, children are transformed from babies into people. With minimal help or direction, normal children arrive at their second birthday able to move around their world, manipulate objects, and make their needs and feelings known. Any group of two-year-olds demonstrates the capacity of the human being to develop, apparently spontaneously.

But the similarity of two-year-old children is more apparent than real; a startling diversity is revealed on closer contact. There was a stage, about forty years ago, when experts would have told us with confidence that I.Q., a supposedly inborn and unchangeable quality, was responsible for these differences. Nowadays, opinion is more guarded. Children are certainly born with a potential, although this is impossible to assess and, the psychologists assure us, never fully realized even in a superbly successful life.

The real differences relate to the individual conditions of the children themselves, and in each case this condition is the product of inherited factors *and* upbringing—"nature and nurture" as the combination is often called. For all working purposes, we can assume that nature has equipped the normal child with all he needs. It is nurture that concerns us, because this is what *we* provide.

What next, then, for the year-old baby who is already used to nursery rhymes, jingles, naming books and anything else that we have wanted to try?

Increasingly, he will want and need to handle his own books, as well as to look and listen while others perform. In fact, the more opportunity the baby has to develop and refine his handling skills, the more cheerfully will he accept the role of passive listener and observer during read-aloud sessions.

It is a sensible scheme, once the baby is toddling, to keep a number of books on horizontal surfaces—low tables and ledges—as well as to preserve some larger, more expensive books by consigning them to the safety of shelves. It should be expected and accepted that the accessible books will be used by the baby. This means that he will sort through them, carry them around, pull some on to the floor to "read" and generally make this book-contact part of his life. This is important; ideally, the adults in the house will have their everyday books within arm's reach, too. At a very early age "passing Daddy's book" can be an exercise that gives both adult and child a glow of shared satisfaction, reinforces the notion that everyone reads and gives the baby practice in visual discrimination.

It is natural for some parents to be apprehensive about allowing their toddler such free access to books. If books have featured in their own lives as objects to be handled with great care, as expensive, luxury items rather than as everyday necessities, they may find it almost impossible to "leave them lying around where the baby can get them."

If you feel like this, try making a connection in your mind between books and food. All parents know that children need nourishing food if their bodies are to grow lithe and healthy.

They also know that older babies and toddlers must start to learn to feed themselves and that this will certainly lead to messiness, waste of food, and even damage to property. Nonetheless, they allow the child to learn; to embark on the bumbling practice, which will lead to that dexterity with knife, fork and spoon that our society expects and demands.

Books are as essential a food for the developing mind as cereal, fruit and vegetables are for the growing body. In an environment where books are valued and used, competence is achieved early.

When Anthony was exactly thirteen months old, his mother wrote in her diary: "Today, for the first time, I saw Anthony go through a book turning over one page at a time. Formerly, he has turned several together, with the occasional separate one. He seemed to know exactly what he was doing . . ." The day before, he had, for the first time, spontaneously "spoken" a word from the text. Opening *The Animals of Farmer Jones* at random, he had come upon the picture of the cow, underneath which is written:

Moo, moo, says the cow.
I am very hungry.

"Moo-oo," said Anthony, gazing earnestly at the page. Later, his mother asked him to "go and get your book about Farmer Jones." He found it, even though the floor was littered with books, and brought it across the room for her to read to him.

Of course there will be some damage, even the odd catastrophe. We still talk about the time one of our own staggering babies hurled not one but *two* valued picture books into the bath where his older sister was being scrubbed! He had the best of intentions, we assured our tearful daughter. He knew she loved those books! Expectation of wear and tear is part of the contract we all make when we embark on parenthood. Why should books—essential family equipment—be seen as different in some way? Or, even worse, as unnecessary equipment!

Recollection of my own family's involvement with books convinces me that books are surprisingly durable, given minimal adult supervision. Somehow, years after the dolls and cars and tricycles have all disappeared, there are Mike Mulligan, Little Tim and Babar standing shoulder to shoulder on the shelf, welcoming the renewed life that visiting grandchildren offer.

"Little books for little hands" is a maxim worth testing at this point. It is almost impossible for a baby to turn a large page without some damage, whereas a small, squarish leaf seems to flip over safely. The Pieńkowski and Bruna titles mentioned earlier are heaven-sent for beginning book-handlers, and there are several other series worth investigating. The best of these are listed at the end of this, or the next chapter. Series should never be used indiscriminately, however. Often, the standard varies surprisingly from book to book, and levels are similarly unreliable. The titles may appear to be of equal difficulty, and yet be widely different in the demands they make on a child's understanding and maturity.

When considering material for this early age group, it is as well to recognize the distinction between theme and story books. Stories, for any age group, have narrative; the characters are established, and then the action starts. There is a plot, with some sort of climax and resolution, and it is necessary for the reader to carry the action step by step in his mind as the tale unfolds. This requires considerable mental expertise, and this expertise cannot be assumed to be present automatically. Why should we imagine that the baby of fifteen months will naturally know that the teddy bear on the second page of the book is the same teddy bear as appeared on the first? I learned this early; "More teddy bear!" (meaning another teddy bear, or rabbit, or puppy or whatever) said my first child every time I turned the page. This was the same child who, at three (see Chapter 4) was dismayed and upset by the apparent disappearance of Patapon the sheep's seven little lambs. For some children, what is pictured is real, always.

Theme books are less demanding, but are still a step ahead of naming books, which depict unconnected objects as *I See a Lot of Things* by Dean Hay. A theme book depicts objects, activities, and situations that are connected in some way. Pieńkowski's *Sizes* with, on successive pages, "big lady, little boy," "big whale, little fish," "big mountain, little hill," is a good example, as are the other titles in this series. In each, a theme is explored, but the reader does not need to know what went before to make sense of any one opening.

A rather special theme book deserves mention at this stage. If your baby is adopted, you would do well to pave the way for later explanation and discussion with a splendid little book aimed squarely at the smallest listener. *I Am Adopted* by Susan Lapsley is a tiny book, with realistic, simple but appealing illustrations by Michael Charlton. Its intention is merely to familiarize the child with the word "adopted." Nothing is more certain than that adopted children hear this term long before anyone thinks they are old enough to understand. Not understand, perhaps, but old enough to feel apprehensive about labelling . . . This little volume puts adoption clearly on the credit side of the balance sheet.

> My name is Charles.
> I am adopted.

says a confident little boy, looking at a book in bed, with his teddy at his side. Later, riding his tricycle with verve,

> Do you know what adopted means?
> I do.

Charles and his small sister Sophie live a warm and happy family life, with parents, friends, a dog, a doting Granny, a rabbit . . .

It means we were given to Mummy and Daddy
when we were little.
And they brought us home to make a family.

Adoption here is equated with belonging; with being loved,
and having fun. Association of ideas is important. Be sure, if your
child is adopted, that he *feels* good about it from the earliest days.
The sensation will cling, when he begins to understand. (For
your own delectation, examine both front and back endpapers of
I am Adopted. They tell a mute but eloquent story.)

Another theme which is likely to demand coverage at this
(or any other) time in your child's life, is the imminence of a new
brother or sister. It is desirable to try to prepare the child for
this intrusion, however young he may be; and a book *always*
helps.

The New Baby by Althea will be enjoyed in its own right,
and, with repeated readings, may even entrench the notion that
the family really is about to be increased, that the newcomer is
inside Mum at the moment, and that good as well as bad features
may be expected to characterize his or her arrival. There is a picture of a doctor examining a recumbent expectant mum's bulge,
and another of her breastfeeding the baby. Nothing more explicit
is shown or described; the rest of the book deals with the care of
the baby, and its assimilation into the family's pattern of life.

There is a useful category of books that sits on the fence between the pure theme book and the true story. It has a confident
foot in each field, and is indispensable as a launching pad for
story proper. One might perhaps call these descriptive books.

Lenski's *Papa Small*, first published in 1951, is the perfect
example. The Small family—Papa, Mama, Paul, Polly and Baby
Small—live squarely (an adjective exactly describing both their
physical appearance and their way of life) in "a big house on a
hill." The Small's daily and weekly routine is mundane to the
point of roaring boredom—but then, the exotic has little place in

the toddler's life, and he recognizes himself, his family and his regular round in this comfortable little slice of life.

Thomas Is Little by Gunilla Wolde betrays its modern origin in its conscious teaching of adjectives, but is a simple and attractive little book of the same kind. It describes a small boy's equipment and activities. Thomas's teddy is "warm, squashy and *soft*," whereas his wooden truck is "*hard* and red and shiny." Other Thomas books are similarly useful, though several are more advanced in concept. They are listed in appropriate sections. *The Book about Me* and *Teddy's Toys*, both in the Smiler series, are similarly successful with this age group. All are small, easily handled books, ideal for this stage.

You will, of course, come to feel that these simple little books are all very well for the baby, but ultimately a little boring for you. Such parental rebellion is to be encouraged! This is the right time to join the local library, if you don't belong already.

Membership of a library allows you to experiment, and experimentation often leads to the emergence of unexpected truths. Be reckless; bring home anything that you fancy, or want to investigate. You'll have to bow to your child's choice in a year or two, so you may as well have fun while the field is yours. You may find that your toddler's gaze is held compulsively captive by bold, dramatic slabs of color in a book that is still several years beyond his understanding. On no account be persuaded that the text, because it is "too hard," should not be read aloud. Modern research shows that children who are exposed to complex speech patterns learn to express themselves earlier and more fluently than those who are spoken to in careful, simple sentences. But the child's willingness to listen, meanwhile enjoying the pictures and the special feelings of warmth and sharing, which read-aloud sessions evoke, must call the tune. If he doesn't enjoy the experience, your persistence will do more harm than good. But don't form hasty conclusions about what is suitable without trying a variety of types.

A real strength at this early stage is rhyme, and an impressive number of artists have conspired to exploit its undoubted appeal. One can believe that the opportunities presented by "The House that Jack Built" or "Old Mother Hubbard" might prove irresistible to an artist who longed to indulge his passion for color and line, and at the same time communicate with the very young. For freshness and enthusiasm this public is unmatched anywhere. Certainly, both Paul Galdone and Rodney Peppé have elevated the old tale of Jack and his House—malt, maiden, priest and all—to the ranks of high artistic and literary achievement, and Old Mother Hubbard has inspired at least two other superb artists to expand and comment on her frustrating relationship with her poor dog. Evaline Ness's Old English Sheepdog smoking his pipe, reading the news and standing on his head is engaging in his irresponsible dottiness, and a newer version by Mary Tozer is a delight. Where Ness's humor has an elegant, understated quality, Tozer's is substantial and earthy. There is a robustness about these brilliantly colored, well-designed pictures that has a universal appeal for children. One feels that this picture book will endure. Its middle-sized squareness suits its character exactly and reinforces this feeling of rightness.

I can think of no better way of catering for a child's literary needs between one and two than of showing him, and reading or singing to him, as many picture books based on the good old rhymes as possible.

Why are so few modern, rhyming picture books successful? No one knows . . . but it does seem that the old rhymes, which were originally spoken rather than written, owe much of their success to their gradual evolution, each generation of children making its mark. Like pebbles that have tumbled down stream beds for misty aeons of time, the rhyme-tales have had their sharp edges smoothed, their contours rounded. Somehow, children know that they are right: real, not bogus. We have to recognize the evidence for this knowledge while we wonder.

(It must not be thought, however, that *no* modern rhyming picture books are successful. *My Cat Likes to Hide in Boxes*, with Eve Sutton's succession of jaunty couplets about the cats of the world and Lynley Dodd's elegant and understated illustrations is a case in point.)

No artist has been more generous than Paul Galdone in providing the world's children with the good old rhymes in whole-book form. *The History of Simple Simon* (in the surprisingly "modern" 1840 version) is ideal for earliest listening and viewing, with its neat, four-line stanzas and clear, bordered pictures. Equally, *The Old Woman and Her Pig* stands alone in a well-populated field. Here, unrhymed verse demonstrates its power to enthrall:

> Water, water, quench fire!
> Fire won't burn stick;
> Stick won't beat dog;
> Dog won't bite pig;
> Pig won't get over the stile,
> And I shan't get home tonight.

Galdone's illustrations in this book capture the spirit of the rousing old tale, and impart a true individuality to all the characters. The text makes compulsive listening, and "ox," "stile," "market" and "quench" will all be stored up for future reference, as more and more traditional rhymes and tales are encountered. And there is, undeniably, a wholesomeness about Galdone's characters—even the mean ones.

The Life of Jack Sprat his Wife & his Cat and *The History of Little Tom Tucker*, both in their 1820 versions, are brilliantly illustrated; Galdone's design is masterly and every feature of the text is there, to be identified and relished, in the picture. (This is of the utmost importance later, when the child is about three, and it is a fault that mars many an otherwise good picture book).

"Over in the Meadow" is probably the most lulling number rhyme ever composed—and one supposes that it must have been composed originally, though its modern forms are diverse. The factor they all have in common is a wonderfully warm, drowsy contentment.

> Over in the Meadow in the sand and in the sun
> Lived an old mother turtle and her little turtle one;
> "Dig," said the mother,
> "I dig," said the one
> So he dug and was glad in the sand in the sun.

"Over in the Meadow" is not to be missed, and is currently available in two quite different, equally successful editions. John Langstaff's version with Feodor Rojankovsky's delicately detailed evocation of animal and field is my choice; but then, I have used it for countless read-aloud sessions since we acquired our own family copy in the early sixties. (Before this the American edition from the public library had come back and forth innumerable times.) But my judgement may be biased; how could anything be "better" than Ezra Jack Keats's more recent celebration of creature and countryside? The warm colors of a summer afternoon drench the little crows six and the little crickets seven in a haze of peace and plenty, and communicate their glow to reader and listener alike.

At this early stage, rhyme helps in yet another more practical way. Once the baby has mastered the art of page-turning, he will be intent upon demonstrating his accomplishment. You'll be lucky if you *can* read the text before the page is turned! Knowing it by heart is almost essential, and rhymes are easiest to learn. Of course, traditional rhymes are usually known at least in part beforehand.

This is the stage when one-page-per-rhyme Mother Goose books have a clear advantage over the bigger type. *Sally Go*

Round the Sun and Betty Youngs's *Humpty Dumpty and Other First Rhymes* are ideal; and the Ladybird editions are handy for spares, to be kept in car or handbag.

This second year is the time, too, for wordier ABC's and counting books, and there is an agreeable and increasing number of these available.

The Very Hungry Caterpillar cannot fail to delight and amaze. It has everything. At the first two openings, we meet a little egg, which quickly hatches a "tiny and very hungry caterpillar." The rest of the book tells the tale of the caterpillar's increasing and cheerful gluttony, as he eats his way through three plums, four strawberries, five oranges . . . to final repletion. At last, stomachache and all, he builds a cocoon around himself, retires, and after two weeks, emerges as a "beautiful butterfly."

This extraordinary book (which has been imitated but never, of its type, approached in excellence) is simultaneously a counting book, a nature lesson, a painless Monday-to-Sunday exposition, and to cap it all, a manipulative book; the finger-sized hole in each edible object on successive sturdy pages invites immediate exploration. But the whole is more than the sum of the parts. Its impact is sobering in its force. An argument for acquiring the hardcover edition lies in the certainty of its endurance among front-line family favorites for years. *The Very Hungry Caterpillar* demands to be learned by heart. Performance will still be given at five and six, when "by heart" material plays a valuable role in learning to read.

Less spectacular, but just as innovative, is Susanna Gretz's *Teddybears 1 to 10.* Why are teddy bears so enduringly appealing? Successive double spreads devoted to "1 teddybear, 2 old teddybears, 3 dirty old teddybears . . ." with the described characters depicted in color against white backgrounds, sprawling dazedly or whirling dizzily (in a washing machine—nothing Edwardian about *these* bears) enchant utterly. At eighteen months, Sam, my eldest grandson, used to gaze as if mesmerized until the last page, on which ". . . 10 teddybears home for tea" pose for their photograph in a large armchair . . . except for one, who has fallen down the back and is seen as two desperate eyes and a pair of clutching paws. "Peep-bo!" Sam would shout in glee, bringing his face to within an inch of the discomfited bear!

The bears reappear in *Teddybears abc*, in which they are seen "arriving in an aeroplane," "climbing," "dancing," "finding fleas in their fur" and "mucking about in the mud."

Even more contrived but just as effective alliteration enlivens *The Oxford Ox's Alphabet* in which the mundane, if improbable ("Enormous elephants eagerly eating Easter eggs") rubs shoulders with the exotic, equally unlikely ("Untidy unicorns under umpteen umbrellas"). Ferelith Eccles Williams uses color with a joyful generosity. Her pictures have a brilliant clarity, which makes them particularly suitable for the very, very young.

Wanda Gag's *ABC Bunny* was first published in America in 1933, and almost thirty years were to pass before it was issued in an English edition. I hope it has come to stay, and that the harsh economics of modern publishing never dictate its relegation to a smaller format, or the use of less robust paper. This book stands outside and above any argument about size and shape; it is right, in its large (21 cm × 28 cm) format, and its black and white illustrations (which are original lithographs) confound the theory that young children need full color in every book. On each page one large red letter relieves any possible monotony—though it is hard to imagine any other reaction than absorbed attention to the saga of the bunny's day, after a falling apple (A) disturbs his sleep and sends him "Elsewhere in a flash." The only evidence of human occupation occurs in two signposts; the animals are real animals who wear only fur and feathers, and relate in animal ways. "Y" for "You, take one last look" depicts a shadowy child reading in the branching arms of a large Y and introduces a note of intimacy at the very end. An enduring book this, which seems to embrace, rather than make use of, its alphabet structure.

Years ago, I used to read my children the Lear Alphabet which begins "A was once an Applie Pie," from the old *Faber Book of Nursery Verse* (of loved memory). In time I had it by heart, and would often say it without the book, with family chorus supporting lustily. Recently, a new, "whole-book" edition of this alphabet has appeared, illustrated by Barbara Sampson. This little book is startlingly individual. Each separate page is enclosed in a suitably adorned border. The text, with large decorated letter at each verse opening, is faced by an inspired succession of characters: bear, cake, doll, fish—and the great king himself. When he was about eleven, one of our sons came home after a history lesson at school one day and said to me, "We've just met up with Great King Xerxes. I always thought you made him up!" If only Barbara Sampson's dashing monarch had been available for his infant perusal!

There is no "suitable" age for this alphabet. Its appeal is to the senses, not the intellect.

A was once an apple pie,
Pidy
Widy
Tidy
Pidy
Nice Insidy
Apple Pie!

The apple pie on the opposite page, set enchantingly within its ornamented border, certainly fits the description. A toothsomely plump little person wears it as an apron, her red-apple head topped with a tuft of green-leaf hair.

This sort of book illustrates the superior effect of rich, flowing sound over mundane *sense* for babies and toddlers. There is a tendency among publishers to produce, in response to a growing demand for titles for the very young, books that are over-earnest to the point of dullness. We need to remember that the sound rather than the sense of language is all important if the baby is to be "hooked." Later, at nearly two, he will be enthralled by the evidence that life goes on between the covers of a book. Meanwhile rhythm, rhyme and the peculiar satisfactions that arise from sound used resonantly will evoke ready response, arousing an expectation of satisfaction, even joy. Compare Lear's *Alphabet* ("Waddly-woosy, Little Goose!") with "Sally likes to skip. The boys fly their kites." Neither text can mean much to the year-old baby—but Lear's will set his feet jigging and his senses soaring—and bring him back for more!

Several other picture books with themes rather than stories come to mind insistently when I decide to give a second-year baby a present. One of my favorites is *A Bookload of Animals* by Maureen Roffey. In twelve satisfying double spreads, this book uses sixty-three words to state twelve trite-but-true similes: "as Big as an Elephant" . . . "as Slow as a Snail" . . . "as Crafty as a Cartload of Monkeys" and "as Mad as a March Hare." The collage illustrations are memorable; I should like the Dog, in his utter Faithfulness, framed on my wall.

By the same author and of the same ilk, is *Farming with Numbers*. A farming family and a description of its daily life is cumulatively built up, from one farmhouse through five cows (Lulu, Jenny, Daisy, Rosie and Bell) to "ten fields, side by side." The satisfying sturdy characters and animals, stylized and recognizable against their uncluttered backgrounds, can be identified, counted and rechecked by an older preschooler. The toddler will enjoy the repetition and savor the bright, flat colors long before understanding of some of the terms is possible.

But let me repeat, in case you forget! Understanding from the *word* to the *object* is a splendid way to go; a container will be noticed to "look like the milk churn in my farm book" long before your toddler ever sees a milk churn, if he is a city child. And why not? A modern city child may *never* see a milk churn. Why not learn about such phenomena from a book?

All children, whether they live in town or country, know about dogs and cats, and this is one reason for their perennial appearance in picture books. Two books stand head and shoulders above all others in this category for the under-twos: *All About Dogs* and *Nothing But Cats*, both by Grace Skaar. Three words to each left-hand page is the order here, with clear and yet sensitive depiction of one cat or one dog on the opposite page. "Sad dogs and Happy dogs and . . . Lazy dogs and . . . Busy dogs . . ." are all there, gazing mournfully, leaping joyously, and digging industriously. That they all say, "BOW-WOW!" ties the issue up nicely. The cat version is just as good.

But Where is the Green Parrot? is a phenomenon; it does not belong in any category. Each page shows a different background (a train, a toy chest, a table set for tea), lists the objects pictured therein, and asks in capital letters: "BUT WHERE IS THE GREEN PARROT?" There he is, in each case peeping from behind, below, above or through, a unifying and satisfying character, who elevates this book to a level far above the earnest little volumes which in their dismal dozens invite children to point and name, as a way of learning. Thomas and Wanda Zacharias do not hesitate to present their tree "heavy with red apples. . . ," to equip their horse with "tight curls, a blue bridle with yellow tassels, a rider in the saddle with high boots—." But then, they probably had no intention of "teaching" children anything.

There is another comparison to be made between those books which are intentionally instructive, and those which imaginatively represent the world. The former state, page after page, bold, boring and obvious truths about shops, sunshine, school or any other natural or man-made phenomenon. The latter establish atmosphere through interrelating picture and language, evoking response on several fronts: emotional and artistic as well as intellectual.

The Animals' Lullaby by Trude Alberti springs to mind. The subject of night and sleep is a fascinating one for the young child, and this apparently simple book uses a series of baby animals to lull and enchant:

> Where does the little foal sleep?
> He sleeps in a field.
> All day he has pranced through the grass . . .

Each animal is shown against a quietly colored background. Each is deeply asleep, but "nobody sings him a lullaby" until the human baby, snug in his cradle, is seen.

> His mother and father are singing softly,
> "Sleep my little one, sleep!"

An older book by Margaret Wise Brown, *A Child's Good Night Book* illustrated by Jean Charlot, similarly evokes image and soothes the senses.

> The little fish in the darkened sea sleep with their
>   eyes wide open.
> Sleepy fish.

> The little sailboats furl their sails . . .

These books are about sleep, and night. They are an experience, not a lesson (and experiences lodge in the mind: lessons bounce off, like as not).

And what is *Buy Me a China Doll*, by Harve and Margot

Zemach about? Is is ostensibly about not having any money to buy a doll—but it is also a lullaby, a celebration of loving family life, a cheerful spoof, with—

> Daddy in the horsey's bed,
> Horsey in our Sister's bed,
> Sister in the baby's bed...,

and a triumph for the virtues of rhythm, form, and home-spun illustration. Access to this incomparable book from babyhood will enrich any child's spirit, show him that language lives and that books are worth the candle!

Spend your baby's second year of life entrenching and expanding the book habit you have established in his first year. If you have been really successful, of course, it won't feel as if you are implementing any policy; you and your child will both know, with assurance, that books are indispensable and that the good life you are leading together is immeasurably enriched by their cheerful and comforting presence.

Books to Use between One and Two

Remember to use this list in conjunction with Book List 1 (page 28) and to consult Book List 3 (page 77) for very bookwise children.

● *The ABC Bunny* Wanda Gag (Coward, McCann & Geoghegan)

● *All About Dogs* Grace Skaar (Addison-Wesley)

● (GB) *An Alphabet* Edward Lear, illus. Barbara Sampson (World's Work)

● (GB) *The Animals' Lullaby* Trude Alberti, illus. Chiyoko Nakatani (Bodley Head)

● *The Animals of Farmer Jones* Leah Gale, illus. Richard Scarry (Western Publishing Co.)

(GB) *Barnabas Ball at the Circus* Robin and Inge Hyman, illus. Yutaka Sugita (Evans)
Barnabas, a big red and orange ball, bounces from one circus animal to another: camel, dog, parrot, seal.

> "Who are you?" said Barnabas Ball.
> "I am Cuthbert the Camel. Look at my humps."

Original use of brilliant color on textured paper makes this, and a companion volume (*Run, Run, Chase the Sun*) a visual joy for child and adult.

● (GB) *The Book about Me* Birgit Ginnerup, illus. R. McGrath (Methuen)
A wealth of simple facts, objects and activities for the toddler to examine, identify and enjoy. The first page says "I am three today ..." Ignore this, or change it to "two." This is a second

year book, without a doubt, as are two other titles in this series:

(GB) *Night time*   I. L. Hauerslev, illus. Iben Claute

(GB) *Who's been eating. . . ?*   Gunilla Wolde

● (GB) *A Bookload of Animals*   Maureen Roffey   (Bodley Head)

The Box with Red Wheels   Maud and Miska Petersham   (Macmillan)

What is in the box under the tree in the garden? It is a baby, asleep, and all the animals come through the open gate to inspect her. Mother shooes them out . . . but is obliged to invite them back when she sees how sad the baby is without them. Each page is framed in a brilliant, scalloped red border. These pictures have outstanding clarity and strong, bright color; they are exactly faithful to the simple text.

The Boy with a Drum   David L. Harrison, illus. Eloise Wilkin   (Western Publishing Co.)

> There was once a boy
> With a little toy drum—
> Rat-a-tat-tat-a-tat
> Rum-a-tum-tum.

The boy goes marching, and is joined in turn by "a friendly old cat," "a green spotted frog" . . . and "a furry brown mouse." In the end, a splendid procession wends its way across the last wide landscape . . .

> If they haven't stopped marching,
> They'll be marching still.

Compulsive rhythm and soft-colored, double-spread pictures in which the action faithfully follows the text. Not to be missed in the second year.

● *But Where Is the Green Parrot?*   Thomas and Wanda Zacharias   (Delacorte Press)

● *Buy Me a China Doll* Harve & Margot Zemach (Farrar, Straus & Giroux)

The Chick and the Duckling Mirra Ginsburg, illus. J. and A. Aruega (Macmillan)

Throughout this admirably simple, satisfying book a small yellow duckling gives a running comentary on his own doings ("I found a worm," said Duckling) with his friend the chick chiming in ("Me too!"). All is well until the duckling decides to take a swim. A first story in every way; the pictures are as simple as the text is sparse.

● *A Child's Good Night Book* Margaret Wise Brown, illus. Jean Charlot (Addison-Wesley)

Davy's Day Lois Lenski (Walck)

> Davy wakes up early.
> He brushes his teeth
>   and washes his face.

A toddler's day, faithfully documented. The supporting illustrations follow the brief text just as meticulously. The whole thing brings the small child's day alive, between the covers of a book.

Drummer Hoff Barbara Emberley, illus. Ed Emberley (Prentice-Hall)

> Sergeant Chowder
> brought the powder,
> Corporal Farrell
> brought the barrel ...

The traditional story of the building of a cannon.

> ... but Drummer Hoff fired it off.

The final explosion is magnificent in red, blue, purple and yellow—and calls for human sound effects. (The one-year-old will be none the worse for his ignorance about what's going on!)

Each Peach Pear Plum Allan & Janet Ahlberg (Viking Press)
An "I Spy" book in which the child is invited to find familiar nursery rhyme characters hiding in the deftly drawn and neatly framed illustrations.

> Tom Thumb in the cupboard
> I spy Mother Hubbard
>
> Mother Hubbard down the cellar
> I spy Cinderella.

The interiors are meticulously drawn, the exterior scenes filled with the light of summer afternoons. Each left-hand page has not only text (framed, like the illustrations), but an engaging little picture-heading.

● (GB) *Farming with Numbers* Maureen Roffey (Bodley Head)

● (GB) *The History of Little Tom Tucker* Paul Galdone (Bodley Head)

● *The House that Jack Built* Paul Galdone (McGraw-Hill)

● (GB) *The House that Jack Built* Rodney Peppé (Delacorte Press)

● *I Am Adopted* Susan Lapsley, illus. Michael Charlton (Bradbury Press)

I Can Help Too! Ilon Wikland (Random House)

(GB) *Mia's Doll* Per Beckman, illus. Kaj Beckman (Dent)

See What I Can Do Ilon Wikland (Random House)

(GB) *What Tina Can Do* T. B. Jensen, illus. Anna Tauriala (Dent)

Four small books in the "Oh Look!" series, which describe the accomplishments and preoccupations of very young children. The colored pictures against white backgrounds are unusually clear.

● (GB) *The Life of Jack Sprat, his Wife & his Cat* Paul Galdone (Bodley Head)

● *My Cat Likes to Hide in Boxes* Eve Sutton, illus. Lynley Dodd (Parents Magazine Press)

My Day on the Farm Chiyoko Nakatani (T Y Crowell)
A companion volume to *My Teddy Bear* (Book List 1). Clear colorful pictures and simple text evoke a child's wonder on his first farm visit.

● *Nothing But Cats* Grace Skaar (Addison-Wesley)

● *Old Mother Hubbard and Her Dog* Sarah Catherine Martin, illus. Evaline Ness (Coward, McCann & Geoghegan)

● *The Old Woman and Her Pig* Paul Galdone (McGraw-Hill)

(GB) *One Panda: an Animal Counting Book* Betty Youngs (Bodley Head)
One panda, two elephants, three moose, four crocodiles ... breathtakingly reproduced in collage pictures, which have been embroidered in hand-dyed silks of rich and glowing color. The impact of these pictures is startling; they have amazing clarity and great beauty.

1, 2, 3, to the Zoo Eric Carle (William Collins)
A large, brilliantly colored counting book with an added feature: a small engine chugs along the bottom of each picture, pulling, successively, carriages containing the animals already pictured, in the numbers specified. At the very end, a wide fold-out page reveals *all* the animals and birds installed in the zoo. Limitless counting practice for the next few years—and fun to look at and learn from now, with an obliging adult doing the counting.

● *Over in the Meadow* Ezra Jack Keats (Scholastic Book Services)

● *Over in the Meadow* John Langstaff, illus. Feodor Rojankovsky (Harcourt Brace Jovanovich)

● (GB) *The Oxford Ox's Alphabet* Ferelith Eccles Williams (World's Work)

● *Papa Small* Lois Lenski (Walck)

(GB) *Sing a Song of Sixpence* Mary Tozer (World's Work)
Everyone knows the tune of this rousing rhyme, and, at one line an opening, you can beat your enthusiastic page-turning toddler and make it to the end without suffering defeat! Later, he will savor the exuberant, earthy quality of the landscape-wide illustrations, singing as he goes.

● *Sizes* Jan Pieńkowski (Harvey)

● (GB) *The Tale of Old Mother Hubbard and Her Dog* Mary Tozer (World's Work)

● *Teddybears abc* Susanna Gretz (Follett)

● *Teddybears 1 to 10* Susanna Gretz (Follett)

(GB) *Ten Little Bad Boys* Rodney Peppé (Kestrel)
Ten spirited boys dispose of themselves in the best tradition in this vigorous version of the old rhyme. Peppé's exuberant and colorful pictures are suitably explicit (enchanting title-page illustration shows exactly the right number of pairs of trousers, socks and shirts for ten boys hanging on a line—with shoes beneath).

● (GB) *Thomas Is Little* Gunilla Wolde (Hodder & Stoughton)

● *The Very Hungry Caterpillar* Eric Carle (William Collins)

The Very Little Dog Grace Skaar
and
The Smart Little Kitty Louise Woodcock, illus. Lucienne Block (Addison-Wesley)
(Subtitled *Two Very Young Stories in One Volume*)

The first story is about growth; the process by which a very little dog becomes a VERY BIG DOG. "All About Dogs" fans (see text) will recognize *this* puppy—and they will love the smart little kitty who can do all *sorts* of things that Peter, his master, cannot do. But Peter can ". . . read a book just like this one . . . put on his overalls all alone . . ." and the little kitty, however smart, cannot do these things. Both stories have bright, primary-colored illustrations of great graphic impact; ideal for the under-twos.

Wake Up, Farm! Alvin Tressalt, illus. Roger Duvoisin (Lothrop)
The coming of the day is dramatic the world over; but on a farm, it is filled with wonder.

> Now it is time for the sun to come up, and the
>   sky grows bright.
> First one, then two, then all the birds begin to
>   sing their morning songs.
> Wake up, Farm!

The Wonder is caught in Roger Duvoisin's early morning farmyard scenes. Bright, clear color and simple statement combine to make this an idea book for the earliest listener.

4

When I was Two,
I was nearly new.

One can imagine a six-year-old, in retrospect, feeling with A. A. Milne that two was indeed a "nearly new" time of life.

In fact, the two-year-old has learned more in volume since his birth than he will ever learn again in a similar period. And he is ready for life. He wants to open every door, take the tops off *all* the bottles and press *all* the switches. Successful parents of two-year-olds are identifiable by the ease with which they connive and conspire: to get their two-year-olds into bed, out of the bath, onto the pot, away from the fire, into a jersey, out of the china cabinet . . . They develop a line of frenetically cheerful, non-stop patter, which astounds and dismays their childless friends. It is of course aimed at diverting the young from occupations of their choice to occupations of their parents' choice. Just as naturally, the young resist diversion with vigor and outrage; there is nothing hypocritical about the noises *they* make during the exchange.

The average two-year-old is athletic, voluble and determined. He assesses himself totally unrealistically, and can see no point of view but his own. Other people's rights do not exist, and he has no feeling for the relative importance of different people, places and things. Your best course is to hold on with as much good cheer as you can while he grows a little; and a little growth at this stage takes him a long way. He will, when you have all but given up, start to co-operate occasionally, modify his "crashing through the jungle" lifestyle, show signs of understanding the rudiments of cause and effect, and even be prepared to wait a little while you make him a sandwich.

I have purposely avoided description of his attractive qualities. Parents are inclined to smile through clenched teeth when their two-year-old's friendliness and his deceptive appearance of shining and beautiful innocence are remarked upon by visitors (who are not staying long, and are known to be returning to peaceful, tastefully arranged houses where books and music and good food mingle in pleasing and orderly proportion . . .)

Can you believe that *books* make all the difference?

What the two-year-old lacks (particularly the first child in the family) is color in his life. What *can* a two-year-old do to satisfy his burgeoning need for experience?—for finding out how things look, how they feel, how they can be manipulated—*except* explore the possibilities of his surroundings? His apparently diabolical intentions are, in fact, innocent, and his outrage at our interference (*he* thinks!) justified.

Constant recourse to books has, at this stage, as many advantages for the parent as for the child.

To begin with, book sessions fill in time, and time hangs heavy for both custodian and child in the early days. Granted, the adult has plenty to do, especially in a busy domestic situation, but the deterrent of a resident two-year-old may make productive accomplishment impossible a great deal of the time anyway, unless some way is found to meet his obtrusive needs. And you may as well if you are going to be interacting with him most of the time, make the interaction as pleasurable as possible from your own point of view, as well as from his.

And two-year-old books are fun!

In our family, a habit of taking to the sofa with books and babies after breakfast ("in the middle of the muddle") seems to have carried on into the second generation. By the time those who are departing to school or work have actually left, a break is needed; the toddler has had to defer to the pressing needs of older family members and is ready for attention. Half an hour of his own with his mother and a pile of books will set the tone for the rest of the morning, and make her work not only easier to face, but less interrupted once begun. If there is a baby in the family, it may prove possible to feed him while this session proceeds, thereby ensuring that *his* earliest memories are of the associated warmths of milk and story. And be sure to include a special "baby" book for him, consulting the older child about its choice and suitability. *Feeling* like an older brother or sister can have a lot to do with *behaving* like one.

Don't worry about leaving the dishes, or any other chore undone at this point; nothing is more certain than that the dishes *will* be washed and the next meal prepared, whereas no certainty at all attaches to the inclusion of story-sessions unless they are placed firmly at the top of the list. I've never been able to understand people who doggedly do the so-called "essential" things first. If you have undertaken to assume a housekeeping role, you must, before all else, capitalize on the advantages; you are, after all, saddled with the drawbacks. And the one advantage that you have over most of the working world is that you can plan your work to suit yourself. Train yourself to smile confidently at neighbors' and relations' surprise or disapproval; tell them, if you need explain yourself at all, that you would be ashamed to neglect your children whereas you don't feel emotionally involved with the breakfast dishes! You will get through as much work as they, in the end, and the profits of your good sense will be as obvious to your critics as to yourself. With any luck, some of them, at least, will join you.

A word about the classic notion of "the bedtime story." This is usually envisaged idealistically, even sentimentally: dreamy child and adoring parent locked in a situation of wonder and rapport, with lights low and the rustlings of night all around.

You may achieve this (if you have household help, no other children, taken the phone off the hook, and decided to relate *only* to this child, regardless of your own and other people's emotional and social needs). More probably, bedtime will be a fairly hectic period, with other family members making demands, nerves a little frayed all round, the child himself overtired and crotchety. If books have featured prominently during the day, you will have no need to feel any guilt about deciding to omit bedtime stories from your repertoire, at least temporarily. Once the child is old enough to accept that a story in bed is sometimes, but not always, possible, all will be well; but two-year-olds are not like this. Bedtime requires ritual—so be sure that you *can*, easily, perform the ritual every night before you institute it in an immutable form.

You might also, at this stage, consider looking about your neighborhood, town, or city, for a book group to join. The name and nature of such groups vary (Books for Your Children Groups, Children's Literature Associations, and so on) but most of them are simply clubs whose members share an interest in books that their children might enjoy. Don't feel that you need to know about books already. All groups want, more than any other sort of member, young (or older) parents who *don't know*, and want to *find out* about books for their children. You will have something of worth to contribute by reason of your current dealings with a baby or small child. You are *really* "in the field!" Even if you can't attend meetings, joining is worthwhile. All such groups send out material, accounts of meetings, lists of good books, and the occasional address by visiting authors and artists. The more solitary your life, the more you need to belong to organizations of people who, like yourself, are tied up with child care and concerned about children's needs. Your local librarian should have information about such groups; or ask at the nearest school.

And so to books.

Between two and four the world opens up to the child. Whereas before this time his curiosity was confined to his actual surroundings, he now wants, increasingly, to go out into the world, to learn about everything, to become involved. He is able now to follow a simple story through a book, and involve himself with the characters. At two he will still love his "old" books—repetition is going to be savored for a long time yet—but will need new and different stories constantly. Books like *Papa Small*, *The Book about Me*, and *What I Can Do*, will have shown him that life goes on between the covers of a book. Now he's ready to advance into other situations, to hear about other people and things, likely and unlikely events.

With the growth of wider understanding, of course, many of his earlier books will assume new roles. Pleasure at the jingly rhythm and bright pictures of *The House that Jack Built* and *The Old Woman and her Pig* will be increased as more of the action is understood, and the people and objects tied up with their counterparts in his real life, or in other books.

Stories that are thoroughly successful with this age group are still in short supply; there is a definite gap, at the time of writing, in the ranks of fiction for the two-to-three-year-olds. Its form, certainly, is a demanding one, requiring as it does the provision of characters who come alive in situations that are believable, and action that *happens*—all within the experience or imagination of a human being whose knowledge of the world and its ways is only just beginning to widen.

Fortunately, the few good books around for this age group are extremely good . . . already waves of enchanted viewer-listeners have demonstrated the power of certain stories to enthral, certain characters to take on immortal life. Harry The Dirty Dog,

Mr Gumpy, Jeanne-Marie, Papa Small and Peter Rabbit spring to mind, and serve to emphasize the rareness of the talent that can speak in real terms to this age group.

Harry eclipses all dogs of fiction for the very young. The briskly related activities, which transform him from a "white dog with black spots" to a "black dog with white spots," are rollicking in the extreme; this is how the small "reader" would spend *his* day, given a temporary relaxation of adult supervision. Harry's family is an anonymous group, which exists only to support him, and provide a backdrop to his adventures.

Only Mr Gumpy has a name, in the two books that celebrate his cheerful relationship with a large and irresponsible group of animals and humans (the pig, the rabbit, the boy, the girl). In the first title (*Mr Gumpy's Outing*) they all set out by water in Mr Gumpy's boat; in the second, *Mr Gumpy's Motor Car*, they are packed uncomfortably into a small ancient "tourer." In both books they all (the guests, that is) behave badly, with predictably catastrophic consequences, but all is well in the end ... Mr Gumpy's affability is unfailing. Both stories end with a joyful gathering of all the friends at Mr Gumpy's home.

Jeanne-Marie, her pets, Patapon the sheep and Madelon the duck, and her friend Jean-Pierre have established their power to captivate over a period of years. The text, translated from the French, is more an excited commentary on the action than a narrative. Its capacity to involve the small listener is considerable, and the impact of the clear, colorful, doll-like characters, against their white backgrounds, arresting and satisfying.

In this series, certain titles are more successful than others at certain ages. *Jeanne-Marie Counts her Sheep* (fortunately borrowed from the library) confused and upset my eldest child at first encounter when she was nearly three. She was clearly enchanted by Jeanne-Marie's plans for the seven little lambs Patapon was expected to produce—they are shown on successive pages, in growing numbers. But predictably, the little sheep gives birth to only one lamb, and Catherine was not only mystified, but disturbed. "What has happened to the other little lambs?" was never answered to her satisfaction at three, and we gave up. A year later, all was well. (Catherine's daughter Nicola gave evidence of exactly this confusion, years later. At a little over three she told friends happily, "Our new baby is inside Mummy, and we don't know if it is a boy or a girl. If it's a girl it will be Maria, and if it's a boy it will be Samuel." In due course, Samuel appeared and we all assumed Nicola's total understanding. After all, she was both intelligent and well informed. One day several months later she looked at her mother with tragic eyes and asked, "Whatever happened to Maria?" Obviously, Nicki could manage alternatives *verbally* but not *actually*.)

Early difficulties of this sort are not consistent from child to child. Some (but certainly not all) children are confused by the depiction of only part of a person or object, and most prefer everything mentioned to be pictured, a near impossible undertaking once themes begin to expand. But it is surely reasonable to require authors and artists to give care to such matters; and quite shocking breaches are common. Sometimes the illustrations give the secret away and destroy the climax utterly. At other times pictures are blatantly incorrect, and show characters wearing the wrong clothes: shoes when the text has them barefooted, day clothes when pajamas have been mentioned.

There is some evidence that with the growth of informed criticism, greater care is being given to these considerations. And yet the best of the old picture books—the ones that have endured—have always given meticulous care to the matching of text and illustration. (This factor is, of course, related to their endurance. I remember reading that Margaret Wise Brown, an inspired and abiding author, would change a word in her final text, if need be, to achieve union with her illustrator.)

Other problems are encountered as soon as we move into the realm of story. How are we to know what will terrify and what amuse? We can't; each of us must find his own way through this maze, and none of us is likely to emerge without having turned into a wrong alley, and been obliged to back out hastily! Sometimes we can use our experiences to avoid later traps, but not always, and we run a risk in applying any rule too firmly. One of the greatest of these is that we will transfer our own trepidation to the child by our careful screening of situations and characters. Another is that we will become so assiduous in shielding the child from any situation which we suspect may frighten him, that his literary diet will become more and more insipid as the months roll by. And we cannot tell! I well remember one of my children always turning the page quickly to avoid listening to "I had a Little Pony" (who was "whipped" and "slashed") and just as regularly shouting with delight when we reached "Taffy was a Welshman" in which ". . . I took up the marrow bone and beat him on the head!" Clearly, for this child, violence against humans was less disturbing than violence against animals!

Another of our children, in the middle years of childhood, used to ask me to read *The Little Mermaid* aloud to her and then, halfway through, be so overcome that she would beg me to stop. By contrast, she showed nothing but gleeful enjoyment of ghosts, monsters, and the everyday violence that seems to invade the life of the modern child, regardless of parental vigilance. No conclusions have ever seemed possible in the light of such contradictory evidence.

The child between two and three is almost daily increasing his contact with the world and its fears, as well as its wonders. We cannot know how impression is building on impression to create the individual set of finely tuned reactions which will dictate his tolerance to events, people and circumstances. Certain simple precautions are sensible and easy to apply; beyond these, we must feel our way, using as guides our own sensitivity to the child's response and temperament.

Back to Françoise and Jeanne-Marie. Only *Jeanne-Marie*

Counts her Sheep runs any risk in this excellent series. With the other titles, we are on safer ground. All simple stories are heart-warmingly resolved, and no cause for undue apprehension mars their cheerful progress. The errant Madelon is discovered triumphantly alive at the end of *Springtime for Jeanne-Marie;* in *Jeanne-Marie at the Fair*, Patapon, left at home because "sheep do not go to the fair except to be sold," escapes and, despite the hazards, joins his small mistress in the circus tent.

There is a substantial but jaunty air about the characters in all five Jeanne-Marie books. They give themselves over to un-ashamed emotion. Their behavior is wholehearted. They are never devious or undecided.

These qualities are shared by Mr Gumpy and Harry, though Harry is a purposeful figure and Mr Gumpy a resigned victim of his friends' exuberance. But they all come through to the very young listener as characters who are consistent and dependable. One knows, when the next title is opened, that Harry will em-bark upon another adventure in which his own energetic pig-headedness will lead him into trouble, Mr Gumpy yet again allow his good nature to complicate his life and banish his comfort and Jeanne-Marie once more plunge into some innocent and joyful celebration which, while its consequences may temporarily dis-may her, will always renew her faith in life and its goodness in the end.

This is how stories for the under-threes should be; they should move smoothly in a steady direction to a predictable out-come. The best of them will contrive to achieve a sort of virtuos-ity, which has the adult exclaiming, "Yes. Just right," to himself, the child listening and looking with that intent absorption that is reserved for the rare and superlative experience.

For this is what contact with a fine book can give to a very young child. Through it, he can experience the capacity of good English words to evoke emotion, to create place, and to usher the reader into that place. If this experience is offered him, as a normal human right in childhood, he will expect repetition of it to the end of his life and make sure that it is always available. In other words, he will become a reader.

Illustration interacts with text to produce this effect, of course, but it is the story and its telling on which the book stands or falls. Make no mistake about this. An adult may open a picture book at random and be so carried away by the quality of its illustrations that he must borrow or buy it; but it is the story that will captivate the child or leave him cold. All too often the language of picture books seems to exist for the sole purpose of justifying the binding together of a series of impressive pictures. This may be well worth doing; but why try to disguise the resulting product as a children's book? At its best, the picture book demonstrates the capacity of illustration to support and extend language, and of language to interpret illustration. It is easy to imagine that this will be achieved more commonly when author and artist are one and the same, but this is not necessarily so. Many fine artists, no doubt under the delusion that the short, simple texts they have been asked to illustrate must be easy to produce, have tried writing their own texts and failed. A master hand on both is needed, and producers of outstanding texts for the two- to three-year-old seem to be in shorter supply than able and sensitive artists.

When one person possesses a combination of talents, of course, heights are sometimes reached. This is the case with John Burningham's Mr Gumpy and Judith Kerr's superb story *The Tiger Who Came to Tea*. Here, picture and text seem to, and indeed have, sprung from the one source. Near perfection of form is embellished by clear and expressive illustrations. The pace is exactly right, the resolution totally satisfying.

Sophie and her mother are having tea when there is a knock at the door. Sophie answers it, and admits a "big, furry, stripy tiger," who plainly (but cheerfully) intends to join in their meal.

Sophie is enchanted and her mother admirably calm as the tiger eats his way steadily through all the food on the table and, ultimately, all the food in the house. Her mother evinces growing dismay as excess piles upon excess, but Sophie remains enchanted. In the end, the tiger departs, Daddy comes home, and there is nothing else for it; they must go out to a café. This they do, Sophie consuming a marvelous meal of "sausages and chips and ice-cream." How better could we leave her?

Pat Hutchins is another author-artist who has produced an impressive number of picture books in little more than a decade. Her work is *for* children, in the best possible way. Text and illustration are mutually supportive, language simple and expressive, pictures a celebration of clarity and color.

Rosie's Walk has already become a classic. In twelve double spreads, two single pages and thirty-two words, it describes Rosie the hen's sober and purposeful journey through the farmyard "... across the yard ... around the pond ... over the haycock ... past the mill ..." At each point she is almost, but not quite, overtaken by a fox who is hungrily pursuing her. He, poor animal, is himself overtaken by a series of related catastrophes, unmentioned in the text, but documented in the illustrations (he lunges at Rosie, misses, and lands in the pond, the haycock collapses on top of him, a bag of flour from the mill engulfs him ...) Rosie stomps stolidly on, unseeing.

For fun, read *Rosie* to your two-year-old without mentioning the fox. It is, after all, a straightforward story. Repeat the performance at regular intervals (or as asked), and note the age at which he does notice the predatory fox and his ill-starred antics. You may be surprised, one way or the other!

The Wind Blew won the Kate Greenaway Medal for the year of its publication. For the young child, it is pure joy. Wide landscape pictures reveal, as the pages are turned, a growing succession of people pursuing their escaping possessions—all wrenched from their hands by the boisterous wind.

It plucked a hanky from a note,
And up and up and up it rose.

The last few openings show a mad mixture of jostling people and flying paraphernalia, all of which is suddenly abandoned by the capricious gale. An even more muddled mix-up naturally results. Two- and three-year-olds will love finding and matching people and possessions in these vigorous and detailed pictures.

Good-Night, Owl! is even simpler, and is bound to succeed. It uses noise words and the repetition so loved by the young, and has illustrations of extraordinary impact.

The Woodpecker pecked, rat-a-tat! rat-a-tat!
and Owl tried to sleep.

The cuckoo called, cuckoo cuckoo,
and Owl tried to sleep.

Predictably, Owl, who likes to stay awake at night, finds the perfect way to retaliate ...

Pat Hutchins speaks directly to small children. Her themes recognize their concerns, the limits of their understanding, their natural taste in humor. That her individual art style works so well to support and extend her stories is every child's good fortune.

Beatrix Potter's *The Tale of Peter Rabbit* naturally serves as the prototype for author-artist picture books. Peter is firmly instructed *not* to go into Mr McGregor's garden, does so, is pursued, almost caught, escapes without his "blue jacket with brass buttons" and reaches the sanctuary of home—to incur his mother's disapproval and the punishment of no supper, and bed, with camomile tea. There is a breathlessness about Peter's adventures that is not often matched; certainly, no tangents or subplots interfere with its course and the tiny, now classic illustrations are a new delight and wonder to successive generations of children.

The "well-read" two-and-a-half-year-old will be ready for this and several other Potter stories—and *Appley-Dapply's Nursery Rhymes* is not to be missed at this stage, if not already known. This is a small gem of a book and can be read in three minutes: three minutes of enchantment. Could any three couplets, with facing illustrations, tell a more complete story than this?

> Now who is this knocking
> at Cottontail's door?
> Tap tappit! Tap tappit!
> She's heard it before?
>
> And when she peeps out
> there is nobody there,
> But a present of carrots
> put down on the stair.
>
> Hark! I hear it again!
> Tap, tap, tappit! Tap tappit!
> Why—I really believe it's a
> little black rabbit!

A word of caution about the indiscriminate use of Beatrix Potter at this time. There is a very wide language and interest range among the stories, and some of them have complex and sophisticated themes. *The Story of a Fierce Bad Rabbit* is certainly the shortest of the stories proper, but somehow lacks the cosy detail of the other tales. Before three-and-a-half, I would use only *Jeremy Fisher, Tom Kitten* and *Miss Moppet*, in addition to *Peter Rabbit* and *Appley-Dapply*—and *Cecily Parsley's Nursery Rhymes*, which, while less distinguished in content, has the usual pictures. But do use them! Don't risk overlooking their capacity to captivate, and the opportunity they offer to familiarize the small child's ear with precise, Victorian-parlor language (" 'I am affronted,' said Mrs Tabitha Twitchit."). As an antidote to the banalities of television utterance, Beatrix Potter's easily available little books should not go unused.

Among recent writers, Eve Rice has emerged as an author-artist who knows what children are like. She seems to look at them from child height; her preoccupations are those of the very, very young. At the time of writing, Eve Rice is a young author with no children of her own. How does she *know* what all mothers of large families know—that some children (but not others) can be relied upon to come "all undone" no matter how well they are zipped and buttoned and fastened? The small hero does just this, in *Oh Lewis!* His little sister, Ellie, by contrast, retains her mittens and her hood and keeps her jacket zipped and her boots buckled. Mother manages the sort of weary-but-stoically-cheerful patience that is typical of the best mothers of such come-apart children, and the book emerges as a piece of life for adult and child alike. Another Eve Rice title, *Sam Who Never Forgets,* is classic in its progression; Sam, the zookeeper, loads his wagon and feeds bananas to the monkeys, fish to the seals, oats to the zebra . . . and then induces anxiety in the elephant's breast by departing. But all is well—he has merely gone off to reload his wagon with golden hay because ". . . you do eat *such* a lot—so I've brought you a wagon all your own." Sighs of satisfaction from the elephant, and two-year-old listener-looker! Eve Rice's earlier books established her expertise with small line drawing and muted color; "Sam" demonstrates her capacity to use flat, primary color to convey feeling and relate action.

It is comforting to have Eve Rice in the ranks of modern author-artists. Overcleverness and ignorance of the concerns and limitations of young children are the twin banes of picture books for the rising-threes, and never does her work show evidence of these faults. Custodial figures, whether parents or zookeepers, are reliable, supportive and accepting. Situations are real, emotions basic and recognizable.

Why are there not more modern books which are "just right" for the two-to-threes? In the last seventy years, surely, children have been liberated. No longer are they expected to defer to adults, be seen and not heard, wear uncomfortable clothes and accede to unreasonable demands. Why, then, have certain books, written for the delectation of very young Victorian and Edwardian children never been surpassed?

Ironically, it may have something to do with the modern conviction that the first few years are of major importance for intellectual development. Somehow learning has become confused with fact-gathering. "Let's teach the children the difference between up and down, black and white, fast and slow," many over-earnest educators seem now to be saying. And so we have a dreary progression of series called "Learning about . . ." or "What do I See . . ." or "How Does it Feel?"

I have never had any patience with these books; most of them are as dull as they are demeaning. They may have some usefulness for school beginners, whose language development has been inhibited by their backgrounds, but even here, the superior claims of simple, spirited stories to inform and inspire can be, and have been, demonstrated. And surely, the meaning that emerges from words used in context, and the lift that comes from language which in itself has life, color and novelty, is what such children always need? I would give them only such language—beginning with nursery rhymes and jingles and proceeding by way of *The Owl and the Pussycat* to *Where the Wild Things Are*. To activate the brain, prod the emotions and stir the imagination every time!

Whatever the cause of the modern lack, it is true that many of the most suitable stories for the very young originated in earlier days. An enchanting threesome, the Catland books by Alice

Goyder, all written and illustrated in 1893 but not published until 1978, must be added to the list. Each small, square volume presents in eleven elegant double spreads an episode in the life of a respectable cat family: Mother Grimalkin, Tilly and Minnie. The tone is Victorian. Grandfather Grimalkin, stately in top hat, arrives with Grandmother Grimalkin dignified in fur coat, and Aunt Millicent, frivolous in "blue bonnet with a bow." In turn the family celebrate Christmas, plan and hold a party, and spend a holiday at the seaside. The illustrations are gentle and elegant, and evoke the simple joys of settled family life. The cats wear only token human clothing—a sash each for the kittens, and a mop cap for Mother Grimalkin; occasionally, an apron for house-work, or a fur stole for travelling. The language is uniformly simple but colorful.

> In the afternoon they hunted for mussels in the
> rock pools at the edge of the sea, all amongst
> the slippery seaweed and scuttling crabs.

And on the ice:

> They wobbled and slithered and panted and
> laughed all morning.

Fortunately, some of the most inspired and able illustrators continue to see the point of giving attention to the old rhymes. One of them, Maureen Roffey, has invoked the aid of her husband, Bernard Lodge, to supply additional verses for several traditional rhymes. The resulting books are brilliant examples of that unity of vision and intention that is, sometimes, achieved in a working partnership. I would introduce *The Grand Old Duke of York* between two and three (it will, on its own momentum, keep going for the rest of childhood—and could be used for cheerful sessions with a young baby—but Bernard Lodge's soft-hearted, silly old Duke speaks to a listening nearly-three-year-old, I think).

The illustrations are masterly. The cover tells us that Maureen Roffey has also worked in children's television and advertising and has designed and produced children's toys and cards. No small talent, hers. The same feeling for design and color which renders *A Bookload of Animals* and *Farming with Numbers* so accessible to the very young child, is seen in *The Grand Old Duke of York*. The "grandness" of the theme is well suited by the exclusive use of brilliant primary colors in the collage-style illustrations, with black (boots and busbies) and textured cloth (horse, barn and hen) relieving and supporting. The total effect is triumphant; but the text must be allotted at least half the distinction. Listen to it (the original ten thousand men have been eroded to a mere handful by this stage):

> The grand old Duke of York,
> Had only twenty men;
> Fifteen marching through a farm,
> Were chased off by a hen.
>
> And two were lost in a barn,
> And two were lost in a sty,
> And the only soldier that was left,
> Ran off and waved goodbye.

The Duke is grief-stricken. First he weeps, and then he throws away his sword and gun. But wait!

> The grand old Duke of York,
> He heard a bugle sound.
> As he buckled on his sword and gun,
> His heart began to pound.

He saw them in rows of five,
He saw them in rows of ten,
And they all lined up in front of him,
Till he had ten thousand men.

Rousing stuff this, sung or said, and guaranteed to elicit the ultimate accolade: Read it again!

Ulf Lofgren's *Who Holds Up the Traffic?* is one of a series of four books translated from the Swedish by Alison Winn. All are successful and satisfying but *Who Holds Up the Traffic?* could well become a classic. Ollie and Emma are first seen sitting in their family car with their mother and father. "They are on their way to take a birthday cake to Grandma, who lives in the country." The back of a red bus is visible ahead and this proves to be just one of seventeen vehicles that has come to a halt. Ollie, with parental injunction to be careful, starts out to investigate, pausing to pass the time of day with a fascinating succession of drivers and riders. From angry farmer-on-tractor to anxious excavator driver and facetious motor-cyclist, past tearful bride-in-taxi, philosophical road-making-machine man and frantic fireman Ollie trudges, pausing to discuss the problem with each. Finally, he comes in sight of the head of the line, where "a fork-lift-truck man is looking very surprised." He can *see* what is holding up the traffic.

"An elephant," says Ollie,
"An elephant sitting in the middle of the road."
"Ridiculous," says the scooter man.
"Outrageous," says the bicycle lady.
"She's tired," says Ollie.
"Nonsense," says the old gentleman in the bowler
   hat.
And he tickles her with his stick.

Ollie pulls, the others push ... The elephant gets up and Ollie "rides in fine style to his grandmother's house in the country." A satisfying tale, well told. (An illuminating exercise for those who would educate the very young is to count the learning points in this apparently modest little book. How many types of vehicle, varieties of people, shades of reaction to emergency, are depicted? How many new adjectives emerge, their meaning self-apparent, in this rich and satisfying story? And this is *real* learning—learning that beds down and stays, because it happens joyously, with nothing of duty associated. Anything missed the first time will be absorbed at second reading, for this is certainly a "read-it-again story.")

As his third birthday approaches, the world is opening up to the delectation and delight of the well-endowed child. He is less imprisoned by his own emotional responses than in the past. Increasingly, he is able to defer immediate gratification of his wishes; he starts to see that some things must be done before others can happen. He is on the way to becoming a reasonable being, and this factor will influence the sort of stories and books that he needs.

As his spoken and understood language burgeons he enters a period which, for parents who themselves love books, is the best time of all for story sharing. Some of the best picture books of all time have been produced for the child over three. There is enchantment ahead.

BOOK LIST 3

Books to Use between Two and Three

Earlier books will still be in constant use, and some two-year-olds will be reaching forward into the next list.

'Ahhh!' said Stork   Gerald Rose   (Faber)
Stork finds an egg and plans to eat it. However, he can't break the shell, so the other animals join in. Simple, brilliantly colored pictures show how "Hippopotamus rolled on it" ... "Lion bit it" ... A surprise awaits them all. Economy of text, exact portrayal of action in illustration.

● *Appley-Dapply's Nursery Rhymes*   Beatrix Potter   (Warne)
Other recommended titles by Beatrix Potter: ● *Cecily Parsley's Nursery Rhymes,* ● *The Story of Miss Moppet,* ● *The Tale of Mr Jeremy Fisher,* ● *The Tale of Peter Rabbit,* ● *The Tale of Tom Kitten.*

Ask Mr. Bear   Marjorie Flack   (Macmillan)
Danny needs a birthday present for his mother, and asks his animal friends for help. Mr Bear finally produces the answer—after a succession of false starts which provide opportunity for the sort of repetition that two-year-olds love. This established title (1932) goes on and on ... Its colorful if dated illustrations are new to each generation; its resolution eternally heart-warming.

The Baby, The Blanket, The Cupboard, The Dog, The Friend, The Rabbit, The School, The Snow   John Burningham   (T. Y. Crowell)
Eight simple and satisfying little books, which might be used a year earlier, but will mean much more to the two-year-old. Burningham's illustrations have delicate precision; these pictures say even more than the deftly economical text.

Bears   Ruth Krauss, illus. Phyllis Rowland   (Harper & Row, New York)
"Bears, bears, bears, bears, bears . . ." begins this unique and successful book; and so it ends, too. In between are multitudes of brown bears ". . . on the stairs, Under chairs . . ." All bears are lovable. This is a lovable book. (First published 1948).

● *Christmas in Catland*   (T. Y. Crowell)

● *Holidays in Catland*   (T. Y. Crowell)

● (GB) *Tilly's Party* all by Alice Goyder (Chatto & Windus)

The Circus Baby   Maud & Miska Petersham   (Macmillan)
Like all babies, Little Elephant is lovable, clumsy, innocent, and irresponsible. The chaos he manages to bring about in Mr. and Mrs. Clown's tent is believable but shocking. All is forgiven ". . . because, after all you are an ELEPHANT!" The pictures are brilliant in color and vigorous in style. A longstanding favorite.

Davy and His Dog   Lois Lenski   (Walck)
A small, straightforward "documentary" about the same Davy as "gets up early . . ." (Book List 2, page 53). Mundane, perhaps, but then all of life is new to the two-year-old and this is a "slice of life."

(GB) *The Elephant and the Bad Baby*   Elfrida Vipont, illus. Raymond Briggs   (Hamish Hamilton/Puffin paperback)
This picture book has all the factors most likely to succeed with very young children: a racy text that calls for "performance," an engaging and ever-enlarging list of characters, repetition, and two central figures who are bound to appeal. For good measure, it has Raymond Briggs's spirited illustrations, and a repeated jingle, which will pass into the language:

> And they went rumpeta-rumpeta-rumpeta all
> down the road.

Freight Train   Donald Crews   (Greenwillow)
One cannot imagine a more dramatic way of learning about

colors and the way they merge. A freight train roars through the pages of this book, with "Green cattle truck Blue coal truck Purple fruit van" and finally, magnificently, "a Black tender and a Black steam engine." There is a feeling of movement, of gathering speed, mounting tension; and then the train is gone. A complete experience, accessible to the two-year-old.

The Friendly Bear Robert Bright (Doubleday)
About "Matt, who likes a story . . . The Friendly Bear, who likes honey" . . . and "Wise Grandpa, who lives in the house over the hill." Beautifully clear pictures in black, white and sepia depict exactly what is happening. Warm, reassuring family relationships.

> And in the forest
> The Friendly Bear gave his bear cub a big hug—
> Because that is what EVERYBODY likes.

(For good measure, the male of the species is shown in a loving parental role.)

● *Good-Night, Owl!* Pat Hutchins (Macmillan)

● *The Grand Old Duke of York* Maureen Roffey and Bernard Lodge (Chatto Bodley Jonathan)

● *Harry the Dirty Dog* Gene Zion, illus. Margaret Bloy Graham (Harper & Row)

The Little Farm Lois Lenski (Walck)
Continuously in print since 1944, and unsurpassed for two-year-old farm-lovers.

> In the autumn
> Farmer Small
>   picks apples
>   in his orchard.

> He hauls them
>   in the trailer
>   behind the tractor ...

Farmer Small is Papa Small in thin disguise ... Adults do not always understand Lenski's appeal, but will recognize it in operation.

(GB) *Look Out Michael* Benny Fons, illus. Iben Claute (Methuen)

(GB) *A Trip to the Shop* Gunner Anton Wille (Methuen)
Both of these small, attractive volumes (in the Smiler series) explore themes that will interest two-year-olds: having fun in a go-cart, and going shopping with Dad. Beautifully clear, bright pictures.

(GB) *Mr Bingle's Apple Pie* Anne Wellington, illus. Nina Sowter (Abelard-Schuman)
Mr Bingle's superb apple tree has, ultimately, only one apple left on it. His initially disastrous but ultimately successful efforts to get it down and "put it in a pie" make hilarious reading (and are reminiscent of "The Enormous Turnip" dilemma.) As usual, this artist's pictures complement the text beautifully, and are expressive in their own right.

● *Mr. Gumpy's Outing* John Burningham (Holt, Rinehart & Winston)

● *Mr. Gumpy's Outing* John Burningham (H, R & W)

(GB) *Mrs. Mopple's Washing Line* Anita Hewett, illus. Robert Broomfield (Bodley Head/Puffin paperback)
A line of neatly hung washing rearranges itself entertainingly when a brisk breeze has fun. Pictures of a chicken wearing a muffler and a pig clad in a petticoat are genuinely funny. Simple text, bright color.

● *Oh, Lewis!* Eve Rice (Macmillan/Penguin paperback)

Pippin and Pod Michelle Cartlidge (Pantheon)

A gentle tale of two mischievous mice children who run away from their mother on a shopping expedition and are reunited just as trepidation enters. Tiny mouse figures in a meticulously detailed landscape invite close perusal. An engaging book.

Play With Me Marie Hall Ets (Viking Press/Penguin paperback)
A little girl invites successive animals to play with her, but they run away, until she sits quietly down, and waits. The magic of this outstanding book (first published in 1955) arises from the unaffected first-person text, and the perfectly designed, deceptively simple pictures. (The only real spot of color is the little girl's yellow hair.) An outstanding book.

(GB) *Polar* Elaine Moss, illus. Jeannie Baker (Deutsch/Puffin paperback)
The collage pictures in this simple, beautifully produced book have startling impact. Polar, a white teddy bear, is brainless in the best tradition of bears, and his wild ways soon land him in hospital ("Numb, dumb bear.") But faithful support from his friends achieves wonders, and "... Soon he is limping around on crutches." Heart, head and eye are all nourished by this book.

● *Rosie's Walk* Pat Hutchins (Macmillan)

● *Sam Who Never Forgets* Eve Rice (Greenwillow)

Soldier, Soldier, Won't You Marry Me? Compiled by John Langstaff, illus. Anita Lobel (Doubleday)
This Old English song has travelled round the world and in one form or another is almost universal. Anita Lobel's illustrations in Early American style show the "sweet maid" as a small girl, and this lessens the harshness of the soldier's final retort "For I have a wife at home!" (The little girl is shown being comforted by two plump, middle-aged aunts(!)—and, on the endpapers, happily skipping.) Music for the catchy tune is given at the end of the book. Like most traditional songs, this one can become a happy item in the "by heart" repertoire.

● *Springtime for Jeanne-Marie* Françoise (Scribner)
Other recommended titles in this series: *Jeanne-Marie at the Fair, Jeanne-Marie in Gay Paris, Noel for Jeanne-Marie.* (Scribner)

(GB) *Susan Cannot Sleep* Kai Beckman (Wheaton)
A simple, cumulative story of a little girl who needs first her doll, then her teddy bear and then her toy dog before she can go to sleep. In the end, there is no room for *her*. Clear bright pictures and repetitive text combine to produce an ideal book. (Mother comes to the rescue.)

(GB) *Teddy Bear Coalman* Phoebe and Selby Worthington (Warne)
A simple, direct story aimed squarely at the two-year-old.

> Once upon a time there was a Teddy Bear
> Coalman who lived all by himself.
> He had a Horse, a cart, and some little bags of
> coal.

One day in the life of such a hero—especially when accompanied by bright, detailed, colorful illustrations—makes engrossing listening and viewing.

Tommy Takes a Bath Gunilla Wolde (Houghton Mifflin)
Thomas again (see *Thomas Is Little*, Book List 2, page 56) cavorting in his bath. An occasional two-year-old develops an inexplicable fear of the bath. This book will help—but all small children will identify with Thomas and enjoy his cheerful activities.

(GB) *Thomas and His Cat*, by the same author and (Hodder & Stoughton), is also just right for this age group. (Other Thomas titles are listed in appropriate sections).

● (GB) *The Tiger Who Came to Tea* Judith Kerr (Collins/Lion paperback)

(GB) *The Train to Tumbuctoo*   Margaret Wise Brown, illus. Art Seiden   (Muller)

An irresistible book. Repetition, train noises, a swaggering BIG train and a hardy little train, and a never-to-be-forgotten jingle:

> Slam Bang grease the engine
> throw out the throttle and give it the gun!

Small children play this book over and over.

Walk Rabbit Walk   Colin McNaughton and Elizabeth Attenborough, illus. Colin McNaughton   (Viking Press)

Rabbit, Fox, Bear, Cat, Pig and Donkey are all invited to Eagle's party, but only Rabbit decides to walk. The others, in various vehicles, suffer successive accidents in the best tradition of slapstick. The hare and the tortoise re-enacted! All is well in the end. Neat, detailed, expressive illustrations aid and abet this well-rounded story.

What the Moon Saw   Brian Wildsmith   (Oxford University Press)

A catalogue of strikingly beautiful, richly colored pictures, which present opposing concepts: heavy and light, fast and slow, in a simple story form.

● *The Traffic Stopper That Became a Grandmother Visitor*   Ulf Lofgren   (Addison-Wesley)

● *The Wind Blew*   Pat Hutchins   (Macmillan)

5

When I was Three, I was hardly me.

Your own self, indeed, at three; or nearly so. What isn't possible, when you can make yourself understood with real language, go upstairs one-foot-to-a-step, take yourself to the toilet and pedal your tricycle?

Babyhood is behind; gone with diapers and high chairs and potties. A year ago, the world beckoned and you wanted to run at it, but clung to parental skirts instead. Now you're *there* and it all whirls around you in dazzling color and variety.

To the uninitiated, a roomful of preschool children is just that; the only distinction is between babies who crawl and older children who walk. To the informed, of course, the difference between two- and three-year-olds is almost as marked as that between babies and toddlers.

The parents of just-turned-three-year-olds must be forgiven for assuming, with incredulous relief and joy, that they have now mastered the art of parenthood. This totally civilized being, (their firstborn: the delusion does not endure beyond this point in the family) is clearly the result of their love and care through days of best-forgotten anguish. From here on, all will be well.

They are, of course, on the three-year-old plateau well known to veteran parents. Later, with subsequent children, they will treasure just-three tranquillity while they have it, merely praying that it will endure until rising-four, rather than shattering around their ears at three-and-a-half.

The three-year-old, give or take a few months, does seem suddenly to be all-of-a-piece; to have reached a stage of equilibrium at which conformity begins to be attractive, when giving as well as taking is possible and cooperation positively enjoyed. People matter to him now; new friends are savored; toys are even—joy unbounding to the adult in his life!—*shared*. It is as if he suddenly stops shouting "No! No!" and flinging himself on the floor (or whatever form his own particular brand of protest once assumed) and says, clear-eyed and interested, "Yes, yes!"

The emerging capacity to cope with his life physically accounts for much of the three-year-old's feeling of well-being, of course. Whereas the two-year-old runs *into* things, almost as if he counts on sofas and people to stop his blundering progress, the three-year-old moves with agility and dexterity. He can dodge, turn, and wheel about in mid-flight. Think what this means to him in terms of play possibilities! No wonder he feels better about the world and its intentions towards him. For the first time in his life he feels—he *knows*—that he is not totally dependent on others for his personal needs. Less need for help means reduced interference. Choice is suddenly seen as a heady privilege.

But it is his accomplishment in the field of language which confers the greatest blessing upon the three-year-old's personality. It is as if "perhaps" has just swum into his repertoire of response, rescuing him from "yes" and "no"—the two terrible extremes. Shades of meaning now start to be recognized and even, increasingly, expressed. All the wonderful modifying words—

later, nearly, tomorrow, almost, wait, half, lend—emerge in blessed effectiveness! But don't imagine that merely knowing such words at two would have made any difference to social behavior. Intellectual development, yes; but not his willingness to compromise. This comes slowly, and is only in its infancy at three; but it is discernible, if you look and listen carefully; the three-year-old has a new understanding of the world and his place in it.

The responsibility of catering for the book-and-language needs of this suddenly superior being would be sobering were it not so satisfying. Ironically, though, it is both easier and harder than before. Easier, because there is such a wealth of material available for the child whose language and experience at last equip him for more complex and sophisticated stories, and harder because he will, inevitably and desirably, become more and more discriminating in his tastes.

He may also, suddenly, demand complete comprehensibility from his books. Whereas before he expected to listen without understanding at least some of the time, now obscurities must be cleared up as they arise.

But there is a wide range of reaction in this area and it seems to relate less to intelligence and book-experience than to temperament. Some children have a precise, step-by-step approach to the gathering of information, and these children will seldom allow an unfamiliar word or concept to pass without explanation. "What's a gander?" "Why did she do that?" "What does slumber mean?"

A prolonged session with such a child may well persuade you that the book in question is too advanced for him. The child, by contrast, may have thoroughly enjoyed the experience. Asking questions and receiving answers may be his idea of an enjoyable book session, even if you find the constant starting and stopping tiresome.

Another youngster of similar age and experience will hear the story out, unfathomables and all. This child may be simply less curious, but may also love the total effect of a story; may be prepared to take details on trust, for the experience of the whole. Our youngest child demonstrated this willingness in extreme form. When only two years old, she would sit in on family story-sessions intended for brothers and sisters of the eight-to-eleven age group, listening almost endlessly to language which must have been often incomprehensible. Even when it was time for the little ones' story, the choice was almost always made by someone else; Jo herself would listen intently, and without comment or question, to anything anyone chose to read aloud.

Fascinating insights into the way language develops have been made in this century. The most interesting of these from our present point of view relate to the sort of environment in which children learn to use language best. Obviously, the more information we have on this score the better.

There is clear evidence that babies and small children profit from an environment in which language is used creatively, to examine ideas, relate occurrences and describe shades of meaning. Far from needing one-syllable words combined into simple sentences to expedite their learning, children need regular access to complex speech patterns if their own language is to develop richly. A truth that is still overlooked, or at least undervalued, is that what a child understands is actually much more important than what he can express at a given time.

Meaning exists in the mind of the listener, not in the sound waves generated by speech, a fact that becomes obvious if one thinks of the uselessness of listening to someone speaking in an unknown foreign language. To keep the comparison going: think how easily children learn a new language if they go to live in a foreign country. Adults often try to learn words, phrases and rules of grammar beforehand. Children, less tense about the business, let the new language flow around and through them, pick up a reference here and there and are able quite quickly to use the local dialect, if not fluently, at least confidently. They don't need lessons on the agreement of adjectives and nouns, or the tense of verbs; they learn by listening, and relating what they hear to meaning, which resides in their minds. Nor do they fall into the fatal adult trap of translating word by word. Children know intuitively that meaning is what matters, and that meaning arises from language in full torrent.

So with their native language. Ideally, it flows around them, rich in content and imagery. From it, and using it, children construct their own view of the world. At no stage can they use, aloud, all the language they understand; their speech lags, inadequate to their insights. The danger lies in adult assumption that because a young child can himself produce only simple words and constructions, he must be spoken to only in speech that reflects this pattern. By this formula, many children are condemned to a meager language diet, fare which makes a mockery of the rich, diverse equipment of their minds.

Attending to children's minds, then, is a profitable pursuit: good for them and rewarding for us. And reading aloud is one of the simplest and most enjoyable ways of providing this enrichment. Direct teaching is boring for children and tedious for adults. But stories, in exciting and varied profusion—that's a different matter! And the third birthday does seem to usher in a period of boundless opportunity in book sharing.

To begin with, it's a suitable time to introduce the first fairy stories. The three-year-old seems prepared to accept the "otherworld" quality of these early tales (the "Beast Fables," they have been called, appropriately). I would suggest for a start *The Three Bears, Little Red Riding Hood, The Three Little Pigs, The Gingerbread Man* (hardly a beast, but of the same ilk), and *The Little Red Hen.* These have in common features that render them suitable for the child whose contact with stories has so far been confined to simple, progressive narratives and straightforward cause-and-effect tales.

It is important to understand the difference between these

stories and the more sophisticated tales, such as *Jack and the Beanstalk* and *Snow White*. The Beast Fables help children to move into an imaginary world which is quite unlike their own, but whose qualities are universal. The characters are often in peril, but the child comes to know that they will emerge unharmed in the end if they are courageous and wise. The rules are rigid; the first two Little Pigs were eaten because they were foolish, the Gingerbread Man because he is, after all, a biscuit, and biscuits are meant to be eaten.

Motive in story is important, and must be comprehensible to the reader. The Billy Goats Gruff want to go up on to the hillside to eat and grow fat. The Gingerbread Man runs away because running away is fun. Goldilocks uses the bears' furniture and tastes their porridge from motives of understandable curiosity. These are emotions and reactions which the three-year-old has experienced himself; there is a two-and-two-makes-four quality about these simple plots that is utterly satisfying.

By contrast, jealousy, revenge and obsession with wealth or power are not, as motives, accessible to the young child's understanding, and this lends a degree of horror to some of the more sophisticated tales. Even though, in *The Three Little Pigs*, the wolf proposes to make a meal of the perky little heroes (and does eat two of them in the best versions) it is in the nature of things that wolves will hunger after pigs—and the resultant context has a rollicking quality that keeps horror at bay. The sustained hatred of the disguised queen for Snow White is a different proposition for the three-year-old; this is a human situation, in which penetrating evil is sensed but not understood; and the unknown and unknowable is always more horrifying than the revealed terror.

Not all three-year-olds will react with fear to the more complex tales, of course, but the possibility needs to be borne in mind. Fortunately, most of them are much longer and more involved than the Beast Fables and their use may well be deferred for other reasons. But some children will encounter them inevitably in story-sessions intended for older children. In this case, you will soon find out whether your child is resilient to their gross horrors or not! And we have ourselves to cope with; I have never been able to bring myself to read aloud any variant of that tale in which a giant, being duped by a visiting family of children which he proposes to kill, slits the throats of his own (eight?) children by mistake. We all have our own tolerance limit, and mine is reached just before this excess!

On the other hand, I am sure that my children met this tale in some form in their own reading; censorship has never been part of the contract for reading alone in our family. It was my own blood that curdled at this atrocity, not that of my robust sons and daughters!

The variety of forms in which the nursery tales have been published, and their occurrence in collections and series at every level from mass market up, makes choosing the appropriate version for the young child a baffling task. Fortunately the field has attracted a number of responsible and sensitive authors and artists, and the best versions tend to stay in print because they are successful.

William Stobbs and Paul Galdone are the outstanding names in the field, and it is not possible to differentiate between them except in terms of personal preference. You may like Stobbs's rough-hewn interiors, his precisely depicted, well-proportioned animals and humans and his rich, deep colors, or you may prefer Galdone's very different treatment of setting and character. From Galdone's big, handsome *The Three Bears*, Goldilocks emerges, startlingly, as an individual, plain in person and brash in behavior. In his similarly spectacular *The Three Billy Goats Gruff*, the dreaded troll has such presence and personality that one almost wishes he might avoid disaster. (One of my grandchildren at three-and-a-half always responded soberly, if not sadly to the troll's well-deserved end. For this child, Galdone's rascally imp was the hero of the piece, never the villain.)

As for the retellings themselves, always be sure, even with a recommended version, that you are happy with the details before reading it aloud. In the original version of *Little Red Riding Hood* (illustrated strikingly by William Stobbs in the Bodley Head edition), both small heroine and her grandmother are gobbled up irretrievably before the tale is out. If this outcome offends you, you will certainly pass on your unease to your young listener. It might be preferable to settle for a modified version in the first place—an illustration of the advisability of reading *every* story alone, always, before you use it with a child.

As with nursery rhymes, it is sensible to introduce different versions, buying some and borrowing others. An old friend in a new guise will be greeted enthusiastically, and comparisons made with interest. You will learn much about your child from his preferences if you watch and listen to him.

The "original" tales (if such a description is valid) have been augmented over the years with others of the same type. Many have become classics, and keep turning up in new versions. Long may this tendency continue! A new author or artist contributes something of his own—a comment, an emphasis, a touch of humor in an unexpected place—and the tale is revitalized.

Such a tale is that of *The Enormous Turnip*. I remember loving it from my own childhood, when I met it in a school reader. This must have been a meticulous, blow-by-blow account, because I have always been faintly disapproving of the brevity of Helen Oxenbury's *The Great Big Enormous Turnip*, despite its obvious success with three-year-olds. And I will not have any version which does not end with, "And they all had turnip soup for supper." I add it, if it is not there. An older, wordier version by Anita Hewett, illustrated by Margery Gill, *The Tale of the Turnip*, continues to be in successful use in our family. Here, the detail is rich and repetitive. "The little old man, the grandfather, the little old woman, the grandmother, and the little girl, the grandchild" together with their friends and the little black cat and the little brown mouse exert an almost hypnotic effect on reader and listener alike.

A word here, about black and white as opposed to color in picture books.

I suspect that many of the adults who demand full color in the books they buy for very young children have not looked very closely at the way these children react to their books. To begin with, a picture book will stand or fall in a young listener-looker's estimation on the story, and the way in which the illustrations support and interpret it. This bears repeating. *Story* comes first, with all its requirements: appropriate theme, well-shaped plot, characters who are sympathetic and who come alive, well-paced narrative, which moves smoothly to a climax—and that elusive quality of "wholeness," which is impossible to define but easy to recognize.

It is true that a five- or six-year-old who is introduced to books for the first time is more likely to be captured by bright red and blue than sober black and white. This, of course, proves only that an unsophisticated taste in any field demands impact rather than subtlety for its satisfaction (Disney rather than Sendak, shall we say). As experience widens, and taste refines, the graphic quality of a picture is tempered by other considerations. Sensitivity to line and form and a feeling for relationship develop unconsciously through access to the best picture books, but are unlikely to emerge spontaneously in the youngster whose experience of books has been limited. This child may need—almost certainly will need—wooing with eye-catching color and slam-bang action if he is to be won over to books at all. The bright lights and loud noises of the modern world (even excluding the effects of television) have a lot to answer for in the impairment of the child's sense of wonder.

You may feel, nonetheless, that your three-year-old is unlikely to be captivated by the apparent austerity of black and white. If this is the case, I suggest an experiment. Borrow or buy a copy of a book called *In the Forest* by Marie Hall Ets, and read it aloud. The illustrations are simple and representational. They depict the events faithfully, one line to a page:

> I had a new horn, and a paper hat,
> And I went for a walk in the forest.
> A big wild lion was taking a nap,
> But he woke up when he heard my horn.
> Where are you going, he said to me
> May I go too, if I comb my hair?
> So he combed his hair, and he came too . . .

Marie Hall Ets is an author-artist of classic status. Her books, which first appeared in the 1940s, speak directly to the small child, for her vision is sure. She looks at the world from child height, without posture or condescension. The concerns of the early years are earnest and intense, as well as light-hearted and ephemeral, and she has retained an awareness of these. Her quiet, unspectacular line drawings support this awareness; bright color, one feels, would direct unwelcome glare upon a created mood, which is perfect.

Then try *Millions of Cats*, by Wanda Gag. In this lyrical and shapely tale a little old man sets out to walk over the sunny hills and down through the cool valleys in search of a cat, for which his wife longs. He finds, instead of one little cat:

> Cats here, cats there,
> Cats and kittens everywhere,
> Hundreds of cats,
> Thousands of cats,
> Millions and billions and trillions of cats.

Text and picture are one here; they are experienced indivisibly. The lettering is hand-done, pictures and paragraphs expertly intertwined. Again, one feels that color would intrude. *Millions of Cats* is a unified experience; it has spoken directly to those children lucky enough to encounter it for fifty years, and will surely continue.

By all means make sure that your child has the joy of rich and varied color in his books. But don't deny him the unique experience of word and illustration that are mutually supportive in the particular and rare way of some black-and-white picture books.

To return to traditional stories for the three-year-old.

Collections of stories are to be viewed with suspicion and examined with care. There is no substitute for reading at least one story from the book before a decision is made; and even then, you may find yourself using only two stories regularly from a volume that contains twenty. The main difficulty stems from a factor mentioned already in this chapter: the wide variation in emotional response required by different stories.

Some collections brashly set *The Gingerbread Man* and *Jack and the Beanstalk* cheek by jowl and try to reduce both to a lowest common denominator by the use of a uniform language and style. This practice usually suits neither, mainly because each requires separate, sensitive treatment, with different audiences in mind. Many children are ready for *The Gingerbread Man* at two-and-a-half; not many are ready for *Jack and the Beanstalk* in its best forms until six or over.

There is, fortunately, a collection that can be acquired with confidence for the three-year-old. Several stories will be usable from two onwards if his babyhood has been bookish, and several might be left until four, but Anne Rockwell's *The Three Bears and Other Stories* will be in daily family use for years. This book is actually the equivalent of sixteen picture books. No page is without an expressive color picture, and every single story is usable. There is something especially satisfying about a book that can be taken along on any expedition—a picnic, a trip to the doctor, a long car or train journey—with a guarantee of stories for all moods and moments. *The Three Bears and Other Stories* is a treasure trove; sturdy, not too big, thoroughly companionable.

There is another category that appeals to this age group and must be conceded a place in its literature. It consists of big, lavish volumes, of which Scarry's *What Do People Do All Day?* is probably the best-known example. The books themselves attract attention by reason of their sheer size, color, and apparent value for money. They are full of pictures. Great double-page spreads reveal panoramic vistas of people (or animals dressed up as people) conducting their lives in every imaginable and unimaginable circumstance, against everyday and bizarre backgrounds; going places on land, on sea and in the air. The scurrying little characters are involved in activities and accidents at once wildly unlikely and comfortably familiar. The number of these books grows constantly.

One must be careful, however, for the standard varies considerably. A fashion in any sphere inevitably sparks off a spate of imitation and duplication, and this has certainly been a factor in the upsurge of publishing in this area. These large, impressive books are valuable if kept in their place: as supports to the mainstream of literature for the three-to-sevens, the central current of which is *story*. Certainly, they can widen a child's knowledge of things, activities and places, but their content is unlikely to linger in his mind long after the book itself is forgotten, as a story with real characters will do.

Let's look at a typical "big book"—Richard Scarry's *Hop Aboard, Here We Go!*—and then at a picture book with a transport theme; in this case, Diana Ross's *The Little Red Engine Goes to Market.* Scarry's title is an undeniable feast of moving vehicles; everything from a bicycle to a jet plane swishes, speeds, clangs or roars across its pages. The text confines itself to supporting these constant, almost bewildering scenes of action. Certainly, this is a book to attract the small child's attention; I recommend it heartily.

The Little Red Engine Goes to Market is a more modest volume, cast in the conventional picture-book mold (it was, indeed, first published in 1946). It may seem at first sight to have too much text for the three-year-old—that is, before we try it aloud and hear how its repeated lines and compelling rhythms catch and keep the youngster's attention. We will be bound to notice, too, that the detailed, satisfying pictures hold his eyes as the story builds to a quiet climax.

You may still feel that *Hop Aboard, Here We Go!* is more informative and therefore superior. Won't he learn more from its crowded pages? Aren't facts important? Back to the story and picture book. *The Little Red Engine* presents a wealth of detail about the life of a small country train with all the paraphernalia of railways in general—level crossings, signals, timetables and all. Because the story makes compulsive listening (it will probably be read aloud hundreds of times before its appeal fades), the details will lodge in the small listener's mind. For good measure, Diana Ross's sound and melodious words will charm his ear. He may forget the details of the narrative, but the patterns laid down by the sensitive, rhythmical use of language will endure. He will respond later to words that flow, language that brings image to the mind and music to the ear.

Give him *Hop Aboard, Here We Go!* and its fellows by all means. He will love them, at the right time. But don't expect their jerky, often unconnected captions to engender any feeling for the cadences of English.

In spite of his limitations, few children's authors have ever achieved such widespread recognition as Richard Scarry. Mass-marketing has made him a household name throughout the world. Many parents who are anxious to introduce their preschoolers to books have little knowledge, to begin with, of suitable authors, titles, or sources of information. But they have almost all heard of Richard Scarry!

Scarry began his career as an illustrator in the 1940s, later moving into writing. He can scarcely be termed, fairly, an author; his stories are at best commentaries on what is happening in his pictures. One suspects that this style speaks directly to children who are used to watching television and films regularly. There can be no doubt that Scarry's rounded, jolly little animal-humans, trotting or rushing about their cluttered world, attract and amuse them. Action is the keynote. Character and situation are stereotyped, and reaction is instant, predictable and absolute. Shock, dismay and grief abound and are invariably presented as funny to the viewer, regardless of their reality to the sufferer. In this, Scarry's work has much in common with the comic book or film-strip cartoon. For me, these books are all fairly shallow experiences—not usually damaging, but seldom inspiring either.

A more definite limitation of Richard Scarry's books should perhaps be mentioned. It is an important drawback, because it negates the very quality which supporters claim for his *Busy Busy World*, *The Great Big Air Book* and similar titles: that is, that they increase a child's knowledge of words and concepts and so expand his intelligence. I am not persuaded of this. These books set out to teach, and yet invoke a method which is hit-and-miss, if not slipshod. Facts seem to shoot from the page of a Scarry title like sparks from a wheel; there is seldom any unifying theme or purpose to lead to cohesion. "Does this matter?" you may ask.

In explanation, let me describe a big book which I believe, *is* based on sound learning theory. *What's So Important About. . . ?* by Joy Troth Friedman fulfils all the requirements of its category, as already described. It covers a multitude of topics, has color, humor, action and size. For good measure, it has style—and it is based on an idea that works. Each opening is devoted to one topic, and these cover a wide range; from houses, umbrellas and toes, to balloons, buttons and bath tubs. The different characteristics and uses of each object under consideration are listed and the one unique, unifying quality of each is identified. Here for example, books are under discussion:

> Books are fun to read. There are lots and lots of
> them in libraries. You can read them on rainy
> days—or when you are all alone. You can sit
> on them when you are too small for the table.
> You can carry them to school. Books can make
> you laugh, or make you cry, or make you very
> smart, or sometimes make you go to sleep. But
> the IMPORTANT THING about books is that
> they tell you a lot of things.

Each proposition is humorously but correctly illustrated (the "chair" pages provide extensive information about rocking chairs, high chairs, swivel chairs, dentists' chairs, wheelchairs, barbers' chairs, thrones, folding chairs, inflatable chairs—all in a format that is clearly aimed at the small child and achieves great clarity and humor.

Facts in *What's So Important About. . . ?* are tied by a common denominator. All lights, no matter how different they may appear, "help you to see when it gets dark." This is their essence; their essential quality.

Research shows that young minds need practice *not* in random collection of facts, but in the discernment of common factors, the recognition of cause and effect, an understanding of action, development, result. *What's So Important About. . . ?* provides practice in deduction—*impels* deduction by its subtly presented material—at a very early level. I regard it as a unique book.

"What about Dr Seuss?" is a question that hangs in the air at this point. Is it time for *The Cat in the Hat* and *Horton Hatches the Egg?* Once again, discrimination is needed.

The Beginner Books are a phenomenon. Never before has a series aimed directly at very young children so caught the attention of the average parent. Beginning with *The Cat in the Hat* in 1957, Beginner Books quickly multiplied. New and different authors were recruited to keep the image alive, and they achieved distinction in their own right. Stan and Jan Berenstain, P. D. Eastman, Syd Hoff and others have all played their part in the establishment of a series that is still, more than twenty years later, loosely called "The Dr Seuss Books." The number now available is bewildering. When to start? Which to use? How to judge?

As before, the formula is the same; every title in the series must be considered separately. Several are brilliant, some are good, many are mediocre and a few are downright poor. Again, as in the Beatrix Potter books, the level of required understanding varies dramatically from story to story. There is no substitute for careful pre-reading of each title, with your own child's level of understanding and taste at the forefront of your mind.

Another factor needs careful thought. The Beginner Book series is at its most useful when children are first learning to read. At this stage, there is a shortage of material that is simultaneously entertaining, well-presented, and easy to read. Beginner Books, with their jaunty, repetitive text and funny (if sometimes vulgar) illustrations, ensure immediate attention. Many children seem to need this kind of approach before they are prepared to involve themselves with the printed word, and Beginner Books provide it to perfection. It does seem a shame to fritter these books away during the very early years of life, particularly as a wide variety of superb picture books caters to the needs of the very young child infinitely better anyway. I suspect, actually, the Dr Seuss titles are used with the youngest age group at least partly because they are so easy to come by. Obviously, thoughtful parents need more information about suitable titles, and where to get them.

It is understandable that parents should feel that books about "real" things matter. Life is a serious business, they reason; the sooner the child starts to collect facts, the better. This is true, as far as it goes, but it stops short of a profound truth. In the early years, facts and feelings are not clearly differentiated—and feelings endure longer than facts, at any age. There is a much greater chance that a fact will take root in the mind if it comes in on the wings of a feeling, a stirring of the emotions as well as the intellect.

Similarly, an interest in a subject that is kindled by an imaginative story will demand its own explanation later. As an example, let's look at Don Freeman's *A Rainbow of My Own:*

> Today I saw a rainbow. It was so beautiful that I
>   wanted to catch it for my very own. I put on
>   my raincoat and hat, and ran outdoors.
> Fast as the wind I ran
> But when I came to where the rainbow should
>   have been, it wasn't there.

The illustrations show a dark, smudgy-gray sky against which the rainbow—and the small boy's bright yellow raincoat and hat—stand out in bright relief. Rapturous attention is guaranteed. By all means try to *explain* the rainbow phenomenon to your small son or daughter if you want to. Children catch enthusiasms; we should all try to let them share ours. But don't expect the details to take root in their minds as the feeling of this story will in their senses. Why worry? Not knowing about the origin of rainbows until ten or twelve won't hurt them, and the magic and wonder of such a story will give the explanation, when it comes, an impact that will help it to stick.

One last word before we move on to the big world of the sophisticated over-fours. The factor that must guide you before all others is your own child's reaction to different books—and this may astonish you. It is quite common for a youngster to become almost addicted to one particular title, and to insist upon its repetition day after day, night after night, when all available readers-aloud have passed the point of no return in boredom. Clearly, such a title (and it may not even be a good book by the experts' judgement) is meeting a need that will probably remain undiagnosed. All you can do, I think, is to grit your teeth and keep reading. By all means suggest—and produce—other seductive volumes, but on no account criticize the adored book. It has probably become part of him by this time, and your disapproval could be experienced as a personal betrayal. Anything as intense as this devotion *has* to be seen as important, even if the need, and its fulfilment, are not understood at all. (No use asking the youngster. *He* won't know in his head; only in his bones and all his fibres.)

And be prepared for (but don't jump to conclusions about) *real* individual differences in children. Many three-year-olds are impassioned by fire engines, earth-moving machinery, animals, or a host of other preferences. It is sensible to try to find titles that will satisfy these interests, but dangerous to cast a child in any particular mold. This happens more often to boys, I suspect. The casual onlooker might well have been convinced that Anthony, at just over three, would prefer his *Big Book of Machines* to any other title; his preoccupation with motorized lawnmowers was intense. They would have been wrong, however. *Sally's Secret, Farmer Barnes Buys a Pig, Happy Birthday, Sam, The Trouble with Jack, The Very Little Girl,* all the Jeanne-Marie books, all the tales from *The Three Bears and Other Stories*—he requested these and countless other, very different stories constantly.

An apparent fixation with a particular topic (rather than a particular title) makes it important that you offer a wide selection, taking in both reality and fantasy, and including traditionally male and female topics, for children of both sexes. It is impossible to avoid the suspicion that many supposed preoccupations are cemented at an early age by well-meaning but short-sighted parents. Let's not risk turning all our poets into scientists—or vice versa!

You needn't worry, if your policy so far has been an open one. You will in all probability be panting behind, rather than leading, your youngster as his fourth birthday approaches!

BOOK LIST 4

Books to Use between Three and Four

Many of the books from earlier lists will still be loved, and some children will be moving on to stories from the next, and last section (Book List 5, page 148)

For ease of reference, Traditional Stories have been listed separately, at the end of this present list.

Anno's Counting Book Mitsumasa Anno (T. Y. Crowell)
In this elegant and unusual book, the same wide landscape is seen at twelve successive openings. In the beginning, the scene is empty except for a winding river. Gradually it develops. Through different seasons and periods of time a growing number of people and animals inhabit a landscape that becomes more and more complex. Each opening is built around a number, from 0 to 12. Each has a balanced elegance, its intricate pattern subtly conveying mathematical concepts and relationships. An absorbing book.

Barbapapa Annette Tison and Talus Taylor (Scholastic Book Services)
Barbapapa is an amorphous, indescribable creature who emerges when François is watering his garden. He is well-intentioned, resourceful (he can assume any shape) and friendly. His appeal to children has been established in this title, and several sequels. The illustrations are as important in his creation as the text and are uncannily in tune with it.

The Bear's Toothache David McPhail (Little, Brown)
The bear, discovered outside the boy's window one night, is huge, lumbering and in pain. The boy himself is sympathetic and helpful. An engaging fantasy effectively complemented by its realistic and yet dreamlike pictures, in interesting purplish tones.

103

Blueberries for Sal   Robert McCloskey   (Viking Press/Penguin paperback)
Little Sal and her mother are picking blueberries on one side of Blueberry Hill and Little Bear and *his* mother are eating blueberries on the other. Somehow, mothers and children get mixed. All is well in the end; and the lively action and peaceful atmosphere are sensitively portrayed in deep-blue-and-white pictures. An enduring book (1948).

Caps for Sale   Esphyr Slobodkina   (Addison-Wesley)
Another classic, in print since 1957 (but the story is much, much older). This book illustrates the picture-book recipe to perfection: simple but well-rounded plot, interesting characters, a satisfying climax—the whole supported by pictures that tell the story and are themselves eloquent. A peddler has his wares (tiers of caps, which he carries on his head) stolen by a tree-full of monkeys. He gets them back, by chance rather than good management. This story works, always, even with reluctant listeners.

Charlie Needs a Cloak   Tomie de Paola   (Prentice-Hall, New Jersey/Scholastic Book Services paperback)
"Poor Charlie! He really needed a new cloak." Charlie was a shepherd, and therefore in an ideal position to gather the wool, wash it, card it, spin it, dye it, weave it, cut out his cloak, sew it ... Every step is described simply, shown graphically. In the end, there he is, resplendent in "a beautiful new red cloak!" Never does this instructional sequence seem like anything but the absorbing story it is. Here is non-fiction at its fictional best!

Clever Bill   William Nicholson   (Farrar, Straus & Giroux)

(GB) *The Pirate Twins*   William Nicholson   (Faber)
Two extraordinary books that prove that knowledge of children and their tastes has been around for a long time. (Both were published in the 1920s). Almost breathless texts follow action that makes complete sense to three-year-olds, even if its signifi-

cance baffles their elders. Each is a total and well-rounded experience, provided with a masterly touch.

Corduroy Don Freeman (Viking Press/Penguin paperback)
The story of an engaging toyshop bear who is longing to be bought. As time goes by, he starts to give up hope. But a little girl has her eye on him, and all is well in the end. Corduroy must be one of the most lovable of all lovable bears. The illustrations do him justice; in quiet color, they are clear and expressive.

The Cow Who Fell in the Canal Phyllis Krasilovsky, illus. Peter Spier (Doubleday)
Hendrika is bored and unhappy, until the day she falls in the canal, stumbles onto a raft, and floats gently down to the town. Peter Spier's double-spread pictures of Dutch town and countryside are panoramic, meticulously detailed and utterly absorbing. Continuously in print since 1957, this splendid book must be regarded as a classic.

(GB) *Everybody Said No!* Sheila Lavelle, illus. Nina Sowter (A. & C. Black)
An uproarious variant of *The Little Red Hen*. Mrs Mudd buys an apple tree and asks her large, cheerful family to help her plant it ... water it ... pick the apples. "But everybody said no!" Nina Sowter's illustrations sparkle. A delightful book.

Father Fox's Pennyrhymes Clyde Watson, illus. Wendy Watson (T. Y. Crowell/Scholastic Book Services)

> The sky is dark, there blows a storm
> Our cider is hot, the fire is warm
> The snow is deep and the night is long;
> Old Father Fox, will you sing us a song?

Simple, rollicking, original jingles are here accompanied by detailed, delicate illustrations of fox adults and children in every imaginable situation. Some of the pictures are in comic strip; most employ balloon-talk to keep the action clear. A unique book, to be treasured for years.

Friends Satomi Ichikawa (Parents Magazine Press)
A catalogue of simple activities and pleasures illuminated by the gently precise, warm and yet humorous pictures for which this artist is famous. Three-year-olds, with their emerging passion for making friends, will linger over these illustrations and listen with absorption to the simple text.

(GB) *Grandmother Lucy and Her Hats* Joyce Wood, illus. Frank Francis (Collins/Lion paperback)
A gentle tale about a small girl who visits her grandmother. Together they explore the attic and then have tea. Fascinating detail, rich language, expressive, homely-but-romantic illustrations in full color.

● *Hop Aboard, Here We Go!* Richard Scarry (Golden Press)

● *In the Forest* Marie Hall Ets (Viking Press/Penguin paperback)

(GB) *The Jackson Family* Ulises Wensell (Evans)
There are no fewer than ten titles in this sound, unspectacular but satisfying series. All books concern the Jackson family. At its center are Jenny and Steve, their baby brother David, their dog Smudge, and their parents. A friendly and attentive extended family provides endless scope for homely gossip and entertaining anecdote. Relationships are warm but realistic, text very brief and illustrations colorful and expressive. This series fills a real need both for information and confirmation of everyday family life. Sample titles: *Our Home, Jenny and Steve, Grandma and Grandpa Jackson*.

(GB) *The Joss Bird* Sarah Garland (Faber)
The Joss bird is a rare creature, and she is hatching a chick. Little does she know that an egg-collector has his eye on her egg. He steals it and runs; the Joss bird gives chase; the egg hatches. . . !

All is conveyed in bright, bordered pictures and racy prose, and all is well in the end, the egg collector reforming, and Joss mother and babe reinstalled on their hill. A rattling good yarn.

The Lazy Bear Brian Wildsmith (Watts)
Wildsmith's use of color is incomparable. His picture books are extravaganzas, but are balanced by the earthiness of his subject matter, and the warmth and humor of his characters. Here, Bear (who is lazy but lovable) finds a trolley and contrives to have all the fun of riding in it while his friends (who are mild but not meek) do all the work of pushing. Their ultimate retaliation is effective, without being spiteful. A heartening story, made memorable by magnificent illustrations.

A Lion in the Meadow and Five other Favourites Margaret Mahy, illus. Jenny Williams (Watts)
An outstanding book; on the one hand very simple, and on the other, thought-provoking. The little boy's mother, seeking to dissuade him from "making up stories again," joins him in fantasizing. But *her* story comes true! Brilliant, sun-drenched illustrations support the story magnificently. "The mother never made up a story again."

Little Blue and Little Yellow Leo Lionni (Astor-Honor)
A classic picture book whose qualities may evade the puzzled adult, but will speak immediately and directly to the three-year-old. Little Blue and Little Yellow are blobs of clear color on a white page. They play together happily; but when it is time to go to their separate homes, they have become one *green* blob! A beautifully rounded, happy-ending story, which will warm hearts and excite imaginations.

The Little Fire Engine Lois Lenski (Oxford)
Fireman Small does everything a small listener-viewer could wish: he slides down the traditional pole, races to the scene of the disaster in a bright red fire engine all hung about with ladders and hoses, rescues a little girl and her cat from an upstairs window . . .

Can you wonder that this book has not been surpassed in the "fire" field for years? The Lenski formula again: square little people, wonderful clarity of outline, simple but informative text.

● *The Little Red Engine Goes to Market* Diana Ross (Transatlantic Arts)

The Little Wooden Farmer Alice Dalgliesh, illus. Anita Lobel (Macmillan)

An enchanting book, first published in 1930. The little wooden farmer and his wife have a neat little farm (depicted in detail, in the ornate frame, which is a feature of this book) but no animals. They invoke the aid of their friend the steamboat captain, and he undertakes to get them ". . . a brown cow . . . two white sheep . . . a fat pink pig . . ." Exquisite illustrations complement a well-rounded, satisfying story. A modern classic, surely.

Lollipop Wendy Watson (T. Y. Crowell/Penguin paperback)

A loving, non-stop little tale about Bunny who "wanted a lollipop and Mum said 'No.' " He kept "wanting and wanting" and Mum kept saying "No," so in the end he "took his piggybank and ran down to the shop." Reclaiming him took Mum some time and got her so upset that "she spanked him and kissed him"—and in the end gave him a lollipop. Moralists may disapprove, but three-year-olds, feeling their wings (and Mums, trying without much success to abide by the rules in the child-development books) will recognize real life when they see it. The sensitive, square little pictures are just right.

(GB) *Lucy & Tom at the Seaside* Shirley Hughes (Gollancz)

A perfect day in the lives of two small children, perfectly reconstructed. Lucy and Tom swim, build sandcastles, eat delectable picnic food, collect seaweed and shells, ride donkeys, and go home at last. Warmth, humor and good cheer dispensed equally by word and picture.

(GB) *Mog the Forgetful Cat* Judith Kerr (Collins/Lion paperback)

Mog exasperates his human family. He cannot remember how to get back into the house through the cat-flap they have considerately made him and is forever mioawing outside the window. But in the end, he helps to catch a burglar! This artist's incomparably clear, colorful illustrations tell the story exactly. A most successful book. Just as good: *Mog's Christmas*. (Collins).

● *Millions of Cats* Wanda Gag (Coward, McCann & Geoghegan)

Mrs Christie's Farmhouse Caroline Browne (Doubleday)
Mrs. Christie and Rachel move to the country to find peace, in an old house in an overgrown garden. But the king, who lives nearby and likes to organize things, takes a hand. How he and his cohorts are thwarted by Mrs. Christie's goat, geese, hens and cows makes good reading—and the elegant, detailed pictures in soft color, good viewing. The king is won over in the end. He had never known that "disorganization could be such fun!"

Shawn Goes to School Petronella Breinburg, illus. Errol Lloyd (T. Y. Crowell)
Shawn is every three-year-old starting play-school. He wants to go and he hates the idea, simultaneously. In these brilliant, simple, vivid illustrations, and the sparse text, his agony and his joy come across. A superb book. Just as good is *Doctor Shawn* (T. Y. Crowell).

(GB) *The Outside Cat* Jane Thayer, illus. Feodor Rojankovsky (Hodder & Stoughton/Knight paperback)
"Samuel was an outside cat. He was an outside cat because he never was allowed inside." But he was also a cat of resource and determination; and luck was, in the end, on his side. The illustrations do this robust tale justice; they are clear, bright and, in places, dramatic.

● *A Rainbow of My Own* Don Freeman (Viking Press/Penguin paperback)

(GB) *Sally's Secret*   Shirley   Hughes   (Bodley   Head/Puffin paperback)

All children like making houses, and Sally is no exception. The secret little house she constructs in the bushes is an enchanting place; but only when Rose comes to share it with her is Sally really happy. The pictures tell the story in warm, bright color and careful detail.

Sixes and Sevens   John Yeoman, illus. Quentin Blake   (Macmillan)

Strictly speaking, a counting book; but how cleverly camouflaged! Impossible to describe the form of this unusual book. Suffice it to say that the language is rich, the conception inspired, the illustrations joyful.

The Surprise Party   Pat Hutchins   (Macmillan)

Rabbit whispers to Owl that he is "having a party tomorrow." This piece of news changes by way of "hoeing the parsley tomorrow," and a host of other unlikely intentions—ultimately creating great confusion in the minds of the intended guests. Small listeners will come to see that language must be precise if meaning is to emerge. Humorous, lively pictures in this artist's inimitable style.

Tommy Builds a House   (Houghton Mifflin)

Tommy Goes Out   (Houghton Mifflin)

(GB) *Thomas   Goes   to   the   Doctor*   all   by   Gunilla Wolde   (Hodder & Stoughton)

Three more "Thomas" titles, all reflecting three-year-old interests and activities. Small, sound little books, written with honesty and illustrated with sensitivity and humor.

Tom and Sam   Pat Hutchins   (Macmillan)

This story of the rivalry of former friends, told in minimum text and bold, clear illustrations against a white background is humorous and heart-warming. Tom and Sam both decide in the end that friendship is more important than competition.

Tony's Hard Work Day   Alan Arkin, illus. James Stevenson   (Harper & Row)
Three-year-old fantasy in full swing. Tony's family have moved into an old house in the country. His parents and two much bigger brothers reject his offers of help (kindly but firmly), so he goes off and builds his own house. Their astonished admiration will warm the cockles of three- (and four–five-) year-old hearts. The pictures tell the story admirably.

A Tree Is Nice   Janice May Udry, illus. Marc Simont   (Harper & Row)
An old book that accomplishes more (because it is a good book) than many modern volumes aimed at raising young ecology-minded citizens. This is a tall, narrow volume with alternate black-and-white and colored, double-spread illustrations, and sparse but telling text.

> Trees are very nice. They fill up the sky.
> They grow beside the rivers and down the
> valleys. They live up on the hills.

The simple joy of the illustrations is likely to convince both readers and listeners that trees are, indeed, "very nice."

Umbrella   Taro Yashima   (Viking Press/Penguin paperback)
Momo is a small Japanese girl living in New York. On her third birthday, she receives an umbrella and a pair of yellow rubber boots. But it is summer, so she must wait to use them. The smudgy, luminous illustrations have a dreamlike quality, which complements the text exactly.

The Very Little Girl   Phyllis Krasilovsky, illus. Ninon (Doubleday)
"Once there was a little girl who was very very very little." There follows a list of all the things she was smaller than, and the specially small furniture she was obliged to use as a result. But it

is in the nature of small girls to grow; and this one did, steadily, until she was ". . . big enough to be a big sister to her brand-new baby brother who was very, very, very little!"

The delicate illustrations enchant, and the subject is of universal child interest.

● *What's So Important About. . . ?* Joy Troth Friedman   (Grosset & Dunlap)

When We Were Very Young   A. A. Milne   (Dutton/Dell paperback)

This is the first Christopher Robin and Pooh Bear poetry book and should be available for all three-year-olds. You will have your favorites among the poems, and may want to defer using some until four or five. But a proportion of these verses are so three-ish that they should not be missed.

Where The Wild Things Are   Maurice Sendak   (Harper & Row)

About Max, who sails off "through night and day and in and out of weeks and almost over a year to where the wild things are." There is no better example than this, among picture books, of the power of the best words in the best way, to enchant; or of the right illustrations to support and sustain. Sendak's monsters might be said to have started a monster fashion; but they are themselves unique. Lumbering, benign, ferocious but friendly, they accept Max's domination. Theirs is a dream-world from which he departs when home calls. Max's participation in their "wild rumpus" (which lasts for three un-worded pages) is one of the highlights of modern picture-book art. An unforgettable book; a rare experience.

The Snowy Day   both by Ezra Jack Keats   (Viking Press/Penguin paperback)

Whistle For Willie

Two simple and satisfying stories about a small boy, Peter. In the first, he has fun in the snow; in the second, he wishes he could whistle for his dog Willie, and can, triumphantly, before the tale is out. Keats is an enterprising artist. His work, a combination of collage and vivid color, is arresting. There is a masterly matching of word and picture in both these books.

TRADITIONAL STORIES

The following editions are recommended for three- to four-year-olds. In each case, the story is told simply and well, and the illustrations are harmonious and yet individual. Children will enjoy access to several different versions of the same tale.

Included in this section are versions of the Christmas story, a collection of traditional rhymes, and several folk tales.

● Illustrated by *Paul Galdone*
The Gingerbread Boy   (Seabury)
Henny Penny   (Seabury)
The Little Red Hen   (Seabury/Scholastic Book Services paperback)
Little Red Riding Hood   (McGraw-Hill)
Little Tuppen   (Seabury)
The Three Bears   (Seabury/Scholastic Book Services paperback)
The Three Billy Goats Gruff   (Seabury)
The Three Little Pigs   (Seabury)

● Illustrated by *William Stobbs*
The Story of the Three Bears   (McGraw-Hill)
The Story of the Three Little Pigs   (Bodley Head/Puffin paperback)
The Three Billy Goats Gruff   (Bodley Head)

Cakes & Custard Brian Alderson, illus. Helen Oxenbury (Morrow)
A mixture of nursery rhymes and well-known and little-known rhymes, this is a superb collection of poetry for the young. Helen Oxenbury knows what people are like in all their moods. Her

work complements the choice of verse in this volume magnificently.

The Christmas Book　Dick Bruna　(Methuen)
Simplicity itself, and utterly engaging, is this very first version of
the Christmas story.

> On a dark night long ago, and in a far country, some
> shepherds were keeping watch over their sheep.
> Suddenly a bright light shone on them.

This book is unmatched in its field. The subject is handled sensitively but not sentimentally, and the illustrations have remarkable feeling, as well as Bruna's usual clarity.

The Fat Cat　Jack Kent　(Scholastic Book Services)
A Danish folk tale concerning a cat who eats an astonishing list of
people and animals before his moment of disaster arrives. The
text is jaunty and repetitive and the pictures full of fun and action, in this excellent retelling. All is well in the end, even the
over-ambitious hero living to eat another meal.

The Fox Went Out on a Chilly Night　Peter Spier　(Doubleday)
A superb rendering of this irresistible old song. One is at all times
on the side of the fox and his "little ones, eight, nine, ten," and
surely *everyone* knows this tune! (It is given in the back, in case.)
The illustrations show authentic inside and outside scenes in an
old New England setting. Every viewing reveals another fascinating detail, in this lasting volume.

Go Tell Aunt Rhody　Aliki　(Macmillan)
The old American folk-rhyme, embellished with almost unbelievably glowing double-spread illustrations. Sung or said, the
humor, the rhythm—and the tragedy, unsentimentalized ("the
old gray goose is dead")—will demand endless repetition.

● *The Great Big Enormous Turnip* Helen Oxenbury (Watts)

(GB) *How St Francis Tamed the Wolf* Elizabeth and Gerald Rose (Faber)

There is no more engaging saint than Francis, who loved all animals, and here he has been guaranteed endurance in the affections of modern children. This St. Francis is robust and humorous. He tells Brother Wolf how wrong it is to eat people, and thoroughly enjoys the feast that celebrates his victory of kindness over violence. This old story is one to grow on, and is here very well served, both by text and picture.

On Christmas Eve Margaret Wise Brown, illus. Beni Montresor (Addison-Wesley)

> It was the middle of the night.
> And night of all nights it was Christmas.

This book contains all the wonder that is Christmas for the child; all the anticipation, the breathless hush of the night before, and the joy of morning. One cannot imagine a more perfect celebration of the festival which, for children, is still untarnished.

● (GB) *The Tale of the Turnip* Anita Hewett, illus. Margery Gill (Bodley Head)

● *The Three Bears and Other Stories* Anne Rockwell (T. Y. Crowell)

6

When I was Four,
I was not much more.

When I was Five,
I was just alive.

Understandable comment, in retrospect, but hardly true. The just-turned-four-year-old is much, much "more" than he has ever been before, and certainly "alive"—to any and every experience!

One might describe the four-year-old as launched. He has cast off his three-year-old conformity and, like as not, his good manners and winning ways. He is entering a "biff-bang" period which will exhaust you (but not him), shock the neighbors, and reduce you to frantically consider enrolling him full time at a play-school. Things get broken this year. Confrontations are unavoidable and understandable; the four-year-old is just as sure that he can look after himself as you are certain that he still needs supervision. You are both right, to a degree. He is bursting out all over, and neither you nor he has any real way of assessing where he is at any given time.

He can now express himself volubly, and move about his world with ease, even agility. Every day seems to bring another accomplishment, another small ambition expressed or achieved. He makes his way from buttons through zip-fasteners to shoe-laces; from spoon, through spoon and fork to knife and fork; from talking through singing to whistling. His progress is so swift, so natural that it may be unnoticed by those around him, except in snatches. A member of the family who goes away for a few weeks may be astonished on his return by the youngster's progress.

No one else will have noticed. In fact, he may be scolded for slopping milk on the tablecloth as he pours himself a drink when, only a week ago he would not have attempted this feat at all. What is more, he will now watch, and listen (within reason!) while you demonstrate a new skill. He half believes that it *is* a skill, and not just an adult privilege so far denied him!

His imagination is on the move too, of course, and often runs ahead of his new understanding. Increased experience brings increased fear, and his expanding self-awareness may reduce the extent to which he will demand immediate support from his nearest and dearest. This self-imposed deprivation may lead to loneliness. For the first time, he may begin to hide his feelings; deny them, even to himself.

The four-year-old is beginning to see things from other viewpoints than his own, although he will have no awareness of this developing capacity. He will use it unconsciously, however, to put himself in other people's places, and this may lead to new apprehension ("If that could happen to him, it could happen to me!"). It is understandable that some parents feel that only

happy stories should be read at this time. It is reasonable to suspect that the inclusion of monsters which "roar their terrible
roars" and "roll their terrible eyes," not to mention wolves who
plot to gobble up whole families of unprotected young, will
merely increase the youngster's own fear of catastrophe. Rest assured; it is clear that children harbor dark and formless fears
whatever we say, do, or present to them. Adult silence on the
subject can be just as disastrous as a refusal to recognize developing sexuality in adolescence.

Small children need to know that other people have fears
too, that these are natural and are common to all creatures.
Human beings have always played out their fears instinctively.
The earliest drama, dance and music arose from man's need to
externalize his feelings about himself and his world; to communicate and share his hopes, fears, and joys. We help small children
to do this when we share stories with them, when we show them
that people are not powerless, that purposeful action leads to predictable result, and that hurdles can be jumped, problems overcome. If we look carefully enough the whole purpose of fiction—
of story—can be seen to be underway at this early stage.

The number of titles available for the over-fours is bewildering. To find your way to those which should not be missed
because they are classics, and yet to be sure to include books of
every type, can seem a daunting task. You should certainly, by
now, be making regular trips to the library, usually with your
child. Enlist the support of the librarian, telling him when your
child has enjoyed a book, and asking for further suggestions.
Don't be put off if cooperation is not as forthcoming as you might
hope; no human institution improves until the people for whom it
is provided show that they expect it to give service. Your enthusiasm may well stimulate librarian interest, and feedback about
successful lines for particular age groups will surely be appre-
ciated. Don't hesitate to criticize the authorities if you feel that
the children's section is undersupplied. One young woman I

know earned the librarian's lifelong gratitude when she organized
a group of parents to make representations to the council on the
sorry understocking of the children's department!

You may feel that your brash, somewhat bossy four-year-old
disturbs the peace of the library—and you may well be right!
There was a time when librarians frowned on any interruption to
the almost hallowed quiet of their surroundings, but this was before they realized that if children were obliged to act like elderly
men and women in libraries, they just didn't come. The secret is
to take them to libraries from birth, accepting that baby noises
and later toddlers' grabbing habits are part of the human condition and must be accommodated by the race in general—meanwhile, yourself, reducing your youngster's capacity to interfere
with others by judicious and good-tempered supervision. If the
worst comes to the worst, you can always pick him up, smile
apologetically (but confidently) and make off. One of my daughters was obliged to give up library visiting with her first child
when she felt she could not again face the inevitable tantrum
again. Her toddler seemed to care nothing for taking books home,
but shrieked with rage because she could not take one of the
quaint little stools! After a search, we managed to buy one, and
library visiting began again.

Increasingly, the young child wants to choose his *own* book,
and this poses problems. All too often choice is made im-
petuously, because the cover design appeals. Its contents may be
quite unsuitable, or at best, hit-and-miss for his needs. To a certain extent, this problem is never solved, except by time; but it *is*
a problem, especially if only one or two titles may be borrowed at
a visit. Of course you welcome his increasing independence and
want to encourage initiative. But successful book provision is important too!

There is only one way in which you can lessen the chance of
your child's choosing books that defeat this purpose: by interesting him in the *whole* book, in a natural way, instead of merely

reading the story. Always, from this stage (or earlier, if he is a really good listener) show him the cover first. Run your hand appreciatively over it and read the title and author, underlining the words as you do so. Then open the book to reveal the endpapers. In a picture book, these are usually colored, and often decorated—and are repeated at the end of the book. Through your example, you can train your child to look in turn at endpapers and title page, at which point you can again underline and read the title, author and publisher. You will be surprised at the interest he will find in this procedure, and how quickly he will pick up the expressions "author," "illustrator," "endpapers," "spine," "publisher." One of the scheme's chief benefits is that it can be used to help choose library books. The child will see the sense in examining the book well, if this has become entrenched as a habit. At all events, it will help the process of choice in the end—and his awareness of books and their unique qualities in the meantime.

Buying books is important too. In fact, a research program in England recently established that children who come from families where books are *owned* are the best readers of all. (I don't need a scientist to tell me such an elementary fact, but I am pleased nonetheless!) Unfortunately, many adults never enter bookshops. It does seem as if the habit must start early if it is to endure. You may feel that even more problems will present themselves in a bookshop, where the bookseller must keep his stock in attractive condition for the ultimate buyer. Here again, early visiting is the key. Children soon learn that libraries and bookshops are different—and that the most "different" bookshop advantage is that you don't have to return the book *ever*, once bought. Modern paperback publishing has brought many excellent titles within the means of average families; you needn't fear that a good bookshop will stock only expensive books. But do make sure that your child has the pleasure of owning a beautiful hard-covered edition of a much-loved book from time to time—possibly a title from the library, which he has grown to love.

A well produced book is a thing of beauty. Learning to love such a book for its physical qualities as well as its contents is part of the process of becoming a real reader—a person whose life is enriched by the sight and feel and smell of books.

If he doesn't have his own bookcase by four, I would urge you to provide one. Simple sets of shelves can be made from planks (cut to length by a lumber dealer) supported by bricks or concrete blocks. These have the advantage of being easy to move and reassemble or extend, as the collection grows. If the youngster's very own shelves are right next to his bed, he will quickly see the point of reaching for a book when he wakes up. If only as a means of insuring family peace in the morning, this makes sense!

The four-year-old's scope is limited only by his capacity, which in turn is the product of his experience, temperament and innate intelligence. The range of scope is very wide, and it is easy to draw hasty conclusions about the reasons for differences. It is not difficult to understand the varying capacities of those children at each extreme of the scale; at this early level, when the child's experience of books naturally involves the mediation of a concerned family adult, it is easy to explain the bookish child's tastes and accomplishments. Similarly, at the other extreme, it is all too simple to recognize the tragic waste of human potential that has already taken place.

What about those in between? There are differences, and they must be recognized. It should not be assumed that all children can be transformed into committed readers of imaginative fiction, any more than that they can be turned into gymnasts or carpenters at will. Each child inherits a wide and diverse set of characteristics, which, interacting with his environment and body chemistry, determine the sort of person he will become. Two and two never make four in human development; at best, three or five.

It is essential for the child's best progress to accept him as he is. One child at four will listen endlessly, his eyes glazed, his whole being so involved in the story that the real world around him does not exist. Another will listen only if the subject is one of his favorite topics, and then only in short bursts. He may keep interrupting, and jumping about—almost as if physical involvement is *his* way, and has to be practiced simultaneously if the experience is to be successful. One might almost say that for *this* child, story-sessions, in whatever form he can take them, are even more necessary than for the first child. Left to himself, he might never tap the vital source that is there, in books. And reading is *different* from gymnastics and carpentry, or any other skill. At its very least, it is a tool (think how much has been written about gymnastics and carpentry!). At its best, it rescues the reader from dependence on his own limited experience and thought, introduces him to other people, other times and other places, helps him to see shades of meaning and to discern relationships. No child should be lightly dropped from the ranks of potential readers—and the so-called "practical" child runs this risk. Tragically, this type-casting of children draws its greatest support from the children themselves. Adult attitudes are all too easily sensed and absorbed so that many children cast themselves, early in life, as "physical" types, who will naturally kick balls, bang nails, sew cloth, *instead of* reading.

Why not all of these things? In a world in which identification of "isms" is assuming astonishing proportions, this particular form of stereotyping (typism?) seems to go undetected. As it is universal in application and life-denying in effect, it is surely time we looked at it. It is *surely* one of the great dividers, taking in both sexes and all races.

And so to the books themselves.

The four-year-old will continue to enjoy his old favorites, meanwhile enjoying longer and more complex stories. As his own maturity increases, he will absorb more of the undertones of some stories, using his developing sensitivity to "see" things that once flowed over and around him. For several years, his needs will hardly change, requiring for their satisfaction stories of increasing depth and detail, but similar topic and type. The essential need for illustration will be reduced slightly, but still remain important. Only the need for easy reading books will vary the scene, and the timing of this phenomenon is, usually, in the hands of the educational authorities of the country in which he lives.

The fortunate child of this age group—the child whose introduction to books was successfully accomplished years before, and whose progress has been smooth and satisfying—will be ready, now, for some of the classics: Babar, Little Tim, the simplest of the Grimm and Andersen fairy stories and a whole host of titles, old and new, which will stir his imagination, expand his experience of people and things, make him laugh, and make him wonder.

Rather than extend this chapter to a tedious length (and because there is such a wealth of diverse and wonderful material available at this stage) I have used the Book List to provide details of many of these titles. Remember that this List and the others throughout the book constitute an essential part of the whole. Correctly used—and with reference to the instructions for obtaining books given in the Introduction—the Books To Use sections should rescue you from that "Where do I go from here!" confusion, which I remember so well from my own early parenthood.

I have felt it practical to deal with this two-year period (roughly covering four-to six-year-olds) in one section. The assumption is that, although the four-to-sixes are diverse in many ways, they have much in common and are moving at their own pace through the same landscape.

Without exception, they have a taste for realism. What other people are doing, how it all works . . . four-to-sixes want to know. It would be very boring if this garnering of fact and deepening of insight could be accomplished only through books about people. Fortunately, heroes and heroines can be animals, vehicles, houses—there is no restriction.

An agreeable number of modern picture books do, however, present the small child against a recognizable family background, immersed in the typical concerns of everyday life. *Dogger* by Shirley Hughes concerns the loss and subsequent restoration of a much-loved cuddly toy called Dogger. The small hero, Dave, is independent and sturdy, inclined to seriousness, and rather over-shadowed by his older sister Bella. His family is splendid. They all see Dogger's loss as real tragedy, Dave's mute grief as the an-guish it is. Shirley Hughes draws children's outsides in a way which leaves no doubt about her knowledge of their insides. Her stories are as sure-footed as her illustrations are perceptive. In *Moving Molly*, a small girl's loneliness after the family moves is resolved in the only possible way when she finally, triumphantly, makes friends. These are not small concerns; they are universal. The youngster who meets them in picture and print is involved in human apprehension and its joyful resolution.

Maisie Middleton, heroine of Nina Sowter's picture book of the same name, is of another ilk entirely—saucy and bossy and possessed of a reluctant and exhausted father who crawls out of bed at his daughter's request to get her some breakfast—and makes such a bad job of it that Maisie packs him back to bed (his relief is patent) and cooks herself up a real feast. Adult amuse-ment at Dad's early morning condition may not be shared by the young, but his incompetence will be savored and Maisie's exper-tise relished. She is superb—pictures and text bring her alive in bright, clear color and jaunty phrase.

The same vicarious sensation of "being in charge" is avail-able for this age group in *Phoebe and the Hot Water Bottles*, by Terry Furchgott and Linda Dawson. Phoebe is a small girl whose father, an aging chemist who cares for her alone, can never see beyond hot water bottles as birthday and Christmas presents.

Phoebe ends up with a whole fleet (157!) which she tends with love, nurses in sickness, educates, and takes to the pantomime for a treat. Phoebe is real. She has strength, a finely tuned understanding of her weary Dad's limitations, and real resource in emergency. She runs her own show, does Phoebe, and her book has style. (One of my grandchildren, when consulted about her hopes in the Christmas present stakes one December, said without faltering, "One hundred and fifty-seven hot water bottles!")

Every now and then a book appears that seems to have an almost breathtaking number of successful ingredients. Such a book is *The Lighthouse Keeper's Lunch*, by Rhonda and David Armitage. Lighthouses—particularly set, as this one is, in a panorama of blue sky and smooth sea, with a line reaching to a house on the cliff down which a basket of delicious food comes each day—can hardly fail. Mrs. Grinling's battle to divert the seagulls from their dastardly habit of purloining the lunch is funny in the extreme. The language has individuality, without any dreary intention to teach, and the illustrations are colorful and detailed.

This husband and wife team have perfected a divided-page, almost comic-strip technique to vary the traditional whole-page treatment of their picture books, and this is seen again to advantage in *Don't Forget, Matilda*, a story about a family of Koalas. Matilda is the sturdy, forceful, small daughter whose father looks after her while her mother works. Father is genial and efficient, but both he and Matilda are inclined to forget things. The pages of this splendid book are crammed without being cluttered. Learning points abound, again, without over-earnest intention. Family relationships are warm ("Perhaps a little something would take away the ache," suggested Father)—but realistic ("Well you'll just have to walk."). Attention is guaranteed; action and humor abound. This koala family is a welcome change from badgers and bears, but certainly in the same warm and woolly tradition.

Frances is a badger, and she has already made her place in

children's fiction. Set comfortably in a loving family, with kindly but not-to-be-victimized parents, she comes to terms with night-time fears (*Bedtime for Frances*), the arrival of competition (*A Baby Sister For Frances*) and several other typical apprehensions and reversals. Why badgers, or koalas—or bears—instead of humans? Why not? Frances and Matilda, in their separate small persons, embody all small girls. Perhaps their animal forms allow them to *be* all small girls in a way human form would not? Or perhaps children, who like small furry animals, just enjoy identi-fying with them; the moral is perhaps blurred at the edges, the point taken more painlessly. Minarik's *Little Bear* has this same quality in his dealings with his family. He is all children, perhaps because of, rather than despite, his furry coat and clumsy bear paws. Certainly, these books seem to teach less obviously than some with real-child characters.

I have purposely delayed mentioning two outstanding titles until this point. Both books have a great deal to say to children of four and over, and yet may be seen as more suitable for two-year-olds, because of their brief, apparently simple text. The first is *The Carrot Seed* by Ruth Krauss.

The text in this unspectacular little book is simple to the point of sparseness. What it does not say is as significant as what it does.

> A little boy planted
> a carrot seed
> His mother said, "I'm afraid
> it won't come up."
> His father said, "I'm afraid
> it won't come up."
> And his big brother said,
> "It won't come up."
> Every day, the little boy pulled
> up the weeds . . .

The illustrations by Crockett Johnson show stolid, expressionless little figures, their uncompromising expressions reflecting their pessimistic statements. The little boy is equally inscrutable—but then, he has his own inner vision, revealed when "... one day, a carrot came up, just as the little boy had known it would." There's faith for you—and the courage to do your own thing, and keep your own counsel!

The last picture shows him wheeling his carrot in a wheelbarrow; an outsize monster of a vegetable. His parents and his brother look on, still expressionless. Over-four independence needs plenty of this red-blooded stuff to grow on!

In its less arrogant moments, it needs reassurance, too. Confirmation of parental love, which is unconditional and total, not to be withdrawn now that babyhood is being left behind, manners are becoming brash, contours harshening. *Little Gorilla*, by Ruth Bornstein, speaks to any child who wonders in his innermost heart about his place in the world. It is, in a deep sense, about love and acceptance.

> Once, there was a little gorilla, and everybody
>   loved him.
> His mother loved him.
> His father loved him.
> His grandma and grandpa and his aunts and
>   uncles loved him.
> Even when he was only one day old, everybody
>   loved Little Gorilla . . .

Inevitably, Little Gorilla grows.

And one day, Little Gorilla was BIG!

Here, thinks the small listener, comes the crunch. But

> . . . everybody came, and everybody sang
> "Happy Birthday Little Gorilla!"
And everybody still loved him.

Certainly simple enough in both word and picture for two- and three-year-olds; but speaking most directly to the "launched" over-four, making his way in the world with his heart in his mouth.

As a picture book this has true virtuosity. Little Gorilla himself avoids both the smart alecky and the sentimentalized monkey image. He is engaging but not coy, mischievous but not slick. The book itself is beautifully designed; its impact is immediate and eloquent. Against a soft green background, Little Gorilla, his family and friends come alive as characters of good humor and diverse temperament. The reaction of Giraffe, Elephant and other animals, who suffer (cheerfully or resignedly) from Little Gorilla's ebullience is inferred, not stated. This is a perfect picture book.

By the same token, Pat Hutchins's *Happy Birthday, Sam* touches on a four-year-old concern: the frustration of *feeling* old enough to dress yourself, but of not being tall enough to reach your clothes hanging in the wardrobe—or the taps, when you know you can brush your own teeth . . . The neat resolution of Sam's problem is inspirational. Grandpa's present proves to be a sturdy little chair, which allows Sam to service himself completely, and to sail his new boat in the sink.

> "It's the nicest boat ever," he said, "and the nicest
> little chair."

The title, also, is so triumphantly simple in both text and bold, brisk picture, that you may mistake it for a two-year-old book. But it is a four-year-old book in all its fibres. One knows without being told that it was written by an informed and feeling parent for *her* "turning" four-year-old.

Curious George, created by H. A. Rey, is probably the most famous picture-book monkey-hero of all time. His exploits are horrifying (he makes paper boats out of newspapers he is supposed to be delivering, and launches them all down the river) and hilarious (his crazy flight on a hospital trolley is classic humor). There are seven books about his wild, irresponsible and yet curiously innocent exploits, and this is fortunate; children at this stage are starting to like series. There is comfort in knowing that another book awaits you when the present volume is finished. George's friend and champion, "the man in the yellow hat," forgives and supports him throughout. George never reforms; we all rollick cheerfully through his described and pictured excesses, and emerge the better for it at the end. His curiosity caused it all, and we know that curiosity is admirable . . .

Curious George Goes to the Hospital brings to mind a belief I have about books to help a child who is going into hospital, or having a new baby in the family, or whatever experience the adults in his life feel may upset him. A story that is set against the relevant background is almost always more successful than a sober statement of procedure. One of my grandchildren has spent many months during her short life in hospital. *Crocodile Medicine*, by Marjorie-Ann Watts, a dead-pan story about a crocodile patient who disrupts hospital routine but enchants a small fellow-patient, had her total, enraptured attention when I produced it several years ago. George's hospital adventures have always had the same effect—and Madeline, whose midnight dash to the hospital through Paris streets is brilliantly documented by Ludwig Bemelmans in his picture book of the same name has never faltered in appeal. ("But the biggest surprise by far, on her stomach was a scar!")

And can you imagine any book about the death of a pet

doing better for a bereaved family than *The Tenth Good Thing about Barney?* Erik Blegvad's sensitive, black-and-white picture shows a small boy sitting at a table, forehead on fist.

> My cat Barney died last Friday.
> I was very sad.
>
> I cried, and I didn't watch television.
> I cried, and I didn't eat my chicken or even the
>   chocolate pudding.
> I went to bed and I cried.

His mother suggests that he "... should think of ten good things about Barney," so that he could "tell them at the funeral"—so he does.

> I thought, and I thought, and I thought of good
>   things about Barney.
> I thought of nine good things. Then I fell asleep.

Later, he helps his father in the garden, and learns about the earth, and its relationships with living things.

> "Things change in the ground," said my father.
> In the ground everything changes.
>
> "Will Barney change too?" I asked him.
>
> "Oh yes," said my father.
> "He'll change until he's part of the ground in the
>   garden."
>
> "And then," I asked, "will he help to make flowers
>   and leaves?"

"He will," said my father.
"He'll help to grow the flowers, and he'll help to
    grow that tree and some grass."

It's no use asking me for a book to help a child face, or come
to terms with, the death of a parent. I can only suggest that all
books which are good, honest, loving books have a capacity to
help all people understand that life is shadow as well as light,
sorrow as well as laughter, and that we all have to come to terms
with it in our own way. Human scars heal in the end in a climate
of love, goodwill and good humor. Don't waste time looking for a
particular book in an emergency; the best book will be the one
that diverts, amuses, engrosses, stirs the imagination and warms
the heart. Such a book may well create a climate in which emotion can be expressed, and this is infinitely more important than
"understanding." How can anyone, adult or child, understand
the death of another loved person?

However, there are many occasions in a child's life when a
book may help him to accept or adjust to a particular situation. It
is understandable that parents should be eager to find and use
these books as need arises, but essential that they should be good
books in their own right; not merely "a book about new babies,
going to play school, the doctor, the dentist, the barber" or whatever. *A Brother for Momoko* was so exactly right for my eldest
grandchild when she stayed with me at three-and-a-half while
her baby brother was born, that the experience of reading it to
her was breathtaking. One felt Nicola experiencing that book
with her eyes, her ears, her whole body. It was somehow, in-
stantly, part of her. Such an experience must remain with a child
always, however forgotten the book. Iwasaki's sensed-rather-
than-seen knowledge of, and feeling for, a tiny girl who has just
turned into a big sister is delicately but strongly transmitted,
both by word and illustration, in this superb book.

>He is tiny and soft and warm.
>And he is my very own brother.

Like most institutions in our society, adoption is changing in form. There is a growing tendency for adoptive parents to stay in touch with the child's natural mother—or father, under some circumstances. If this practice ever becomes universal, the need for a special book on adoption may evaporate. After all, it's *not knowing* where you come from, and why your original parents disowned you, that upsets many adopted children. It is unlikely, however, that enlightened treatment of the subject will ever become universal. We will continue to need *Mr Fairweather and his Family* and *The Hollywell Family*, two splendid books by Margaret Kornitzer.

The first tells of the story of Mr. and Mrs. Fairweather, who have a comfortable house, a cat, a dog—but no baby. Their acquisition of small Andrew Fairweather is faithfully documented in the text and in Shirley Hughes's wonderfully warm, human illustrations; the mechanics, the legalities, the human emotions, the settling in, the ultimate adoption of a small sister. The Hollywells are a different proposition. They produce Mary without any fuss and then get stuck. Adoption of George transforms them into a real family, and makes them all happy ("He looks like a George," said Daddy. "He's splendid, isn't he!")

Mr Fairweather, illustrated by Margery Gill, was first published in 1960, and we provided a copy for our own children. Several close friends had adopted children, and it seemed to us that our children's understanding was important, too. It became a favorite immediately. The subject is obviously fascinating, even for children who have no need to identify. Of course, it is a good book in its own right.

So is *Don't Forget Tom*, an excellent "documentary" about a mentally handicapped child. Tom lives in a loving and caring family. His sister and brother are normal, and, with their parents' wise assistance, try to help Tom to have fun, to learn, to cope with his problems. The excellent colored photographs depict a family of real people getting on with their separate lives and accommodating a handicapped member with courage and honesty. This is not a book for the "different" child, but for his sisters, brothers and all other children. And adults too; we have a long way to go before the handicapped children of the world receive their share, as a right.

Facts about human reproduction can be very easily taught at this stage, and most parents will be helped along this particular path by the provision of suitable books. What is suitable? How much information does a child need by the time he begins school for example? Physical differences pose no particular problems in families or groups where there are children of both sexes, and where parents and other adults are natural and un-self-conscious about bodily functions. My own experience leads me to believe that children who have not been made to feel uneasy about the topic will ask questions when they start to wonder. Certainly, the knowledge that babies grow inside their mothers should be given at first opportunity. Even if they have stopped producing children themselves, most parents can turn a pregnant friend or relation to good use here.

A strong case can be made for giving information about sexual intercourse long before the topic has any emotional significance for the child. The details will be received calmly and naturally at this early stage, and will certainly lessen the chance of later shock. But be warned: it is not uncommon for a young child to forget the whole thing, and ask again later. (It is easy to understand adult exasperation with this phenomenon!) Try to avoid books that sentimentalize birth or the facts of sex (this was very common in the literature of the forties and fifties). Nothing convinces a child more quickly that there is something unpleasant about a subject than the adoption of a "sweetness and light" tone on the part of the adults in his life!

This is one area where you must have your heart in your policy. There are good books available, and I have listed some of them in the next Book List. I recommend that you read any book carefully before using it. There is such a wide range of reaction (among adults, I suspect, rather than children) to this emotion-charged topic that you must come to terms with your own views and decide upon a course of action or delay. Fumbling over the text of a book you have not read is not to be risked! (Take heart; your five-year-old is likely to think human functioning matters less than the way Dad's new motor-mower works—or become so bored that you decide jointly to move on to Mike Mulligan and his Steam Shovel.)

Now is the time to introduce the occasional story without pictures. In fact, I feel that the fourth birthday might well be marked by the acquisition of one of the collections mentioned below, or in the Book List. Have you ever told a child a story that you invented as you went—and felt his close attention to the words, almost *seen* the picture he was building up in his mind? This is what happens—what *must* happen—when, later, children read to themselves. They must carry the image in their minds, modifying it, building on it, taking the action a step further ... What better time to start giving practice than now?

To Read and to Tell is one of my favorite books for this purpose. My own well-worn copy bears testimony to the use it has had over the years. In this anthology Norah Montgomerie has collected a wide-range of stories, conveniently grouped under headings: "First Tales To Tell," "Stuff and Nonsense," "Animal Fables," "Stories Round the Year," "Heroes and Heroines," and "Once Upon a Time." Each of the ninety-eight stories might make a picture book, if illustrated; the tales vary somewhat in length and complexity, but many are suitable for good listeners of just over four. Try using one of the shortest stories first, perhaps from "First Tales to Tell." Sandwich your performance between two picture books, if you anticipate opposition to the "no-picture" nature of your chosen story. Say, perhaps: "Let's have a story from this book. See if you can make the pictures in your head."

Don't miss the opportunity to point out the Contents list in the front of the book, briefly telling the youngster about the different sections. He may like to choose the section to be tapped first; in this case, accede to his request, merely choosing one of the shorter stories from the section. It will help, obviously, if you have made yourself familiar with the stories beforehand. You may be surprised at the interest he shows in the Contents pages, and the expertise he develops in finding "his" stories at subsequent encounters. This identification is the beginning of the reading process. As you read a possible title to him, always run your finger under the words at the speed you are speaking.

The Ruth Ainsworth Book, illustrated with occasional black-and-white line drawings by Shirley Hughes, would also be a splendid volume to acquire at this time. Its pages are well proportioned and its print large; it has a generous, substantial look about it, and an attractive, colorful jacket. A book to grow on, this. It contains thirty-six stories, graded in length and level. Most of them describe the everyday doings and concerns of small children, a task at which this author excels. One can read the easiest, early stories to a four-year-old, moving on imperceptibly to slightly longer, more complex stories as the child grows. Becoming fond of such a book, having it always visible, within reach on the shelf, waiting to be read, is part of growing to be a reader.

A variation of the no-picture story is provided by the occasional book that has more text than illustration, or even better, by a rare book which has alternate double spreads of text and picture. Years ago, *The Little Boy and his House* and *The Little Boys and their Boats,* both by Stephen Bone and Mary Adshead, gave hours of pleasure in my own family. These books tell the story of a search for the right kind of house, the right kind of boat. Each, ultimately, provides very comprehensive coverage of house and boat types, and the reasons for their use in different parts of the world. At the end of both stories, house and boats having been suitably constructed, the little boy and his uncle hold a party for all the previously visited boatmen (or house-dwellers) of the world. My children used to compete to match the various guests with their hats (ordinary and exotic) hanging in the hall.

These stories succeed where purely factual accounts might fail, through a happy combination of characters who are real people, language that is clear and well-tuned, and plots that have pattern, shape and climax.

A modern confusion over the role of Christianity in children's lives needs facing, and resolving. Parents who are not themselves religious and wish their children to come to their own conclusions as they grow up, are often reluctant to introduce any stories that have Christian associations. It is a great shame if this reluctance deprives children of seven years and over of the rousing (often bloodthirsty!) Old Testament tales. In the early years, it is the story of the Nativity that is most likely to be omitted from listening experience.

Christmas is an important festival in all children's lives, regardless of its implications; and the Nativity story is one of the most simple and yet awe-inspiring ever told. There is something universally satisfying in the thought of a child who was destined for lasting glory beginning his life in a humble barn, the child of humble parents. Regard it as a legend, a folk-myth if you will, but don't spurn it any more than you would any other legend, because you fear indoctrination!

I would go further, and make certain that all young children grew to know and love the most beautiful version of all, that from the Gospel of St Luke:

> And she brought forth her firstborn son, and
> wrapped him in swaddling clothes, and laid
> him in a manger; because there was no room
> for him in the inn . . .

Why should modern children be shielded from exposure to these pure, easily absorbed, time-worn phrases?

> But Mary kept all these things, and pondered
> them in her heart.

Reducing language to the flat, graded-vocabulary utterances of many modern retellings certainly makes sure that children will not ponder these things in *their* hearts! Why this deprivation, when such a splendid heritage has been forged for them by earlier generations?

Two major requirements of Nativity retellings are dignity and simplicity. Fortunately, there are several versions that fulfil these conditions, and provide infinitely more, while avoiding mention of the divine element in the story. Astrid Lindgren's *Christmas in the Stable*, with Harald Wiberg's moving, luminous illustrations, permits of any, or no interpretation. The child's parents, and the shepherds, wear modern clothing; and the kings do not appear at all. And yet the book has a pervading peace and wonder about it that is irresistible. It was produced in time for my youngest children's pleasure and is still well loved in our family.

Long Ago in Bethlehem by Masahiro Kasuya fills the same role, but is traditional in setting and character. The hazy, softly colored illustrations are very beautiful, and text is sure-footed.

> "Not much of a place for a king," a shepherd said
> softly.
> But Joseph smiled and Jesus slept and Mary was
> content.

But for total, uncompromising involvement in the glory (angels and all), the earthiness, the fear, the incomparable detail (what other baby ever received incense, myrrh, and gold?), Felix Hoffmann's version has no peer. This *Story of Christmas* begins with the Angel Gabriel announcing, and ends with Herod raging, and the holy family escaping. Every step of the story is made memorable by these formal and yet infinitely personal pictures. The baby himself is a Botticelli cherub; his parents dazed by their special role but resolute in their acceptance of it. This, for me, is the best Christmas book ever produced.

And this is the time for poetry! No need, now, to confine yourself to nursery rhymes, with infusions of simple jingle and traditional rhyming story. All these will continue to have a place—but every manner of verse may now be tried.

Under the Cherry Tree, a collection by Cynthia Mitchell, includes verse by a wide range of poets, and is superbly illustrated by Satomi Ichikawa. Such lines as John Irvine's

> And wind and wave and moon and stars
> Shall sing you lullaby.

will start to show the child how simple words can be combined in a way that makes them special. He may not know that his senses are being prodded and his imagination nourished, but he will know that the experience is enjoyable.

A wonderful poem by Olive Dove occurs in this collection:

> What do you choose?
> Coral beads on a string,
> Purple velvet and lace
> And an emerald ring.

What will you have?
Pomegranates and pears,
Jellies, truffles and trifles
And chocolate eclairs.

What would you like? . . .

Here is an early taste of the power of poetry to provoke reaction by the linking of very different objects or experiences; the magical and mystical ("Coral beads on a string . . .") and the down-to-earth and everyday ("Jellies, truffles and trifles . . .") And children love lists. Five verses of delightful propositions are sure to be listened to with absorption and pleasure.

It is in the nature of children's poetry to be repeated and repeated, and this is a good argument for owning at least one "big" anthology. Children take great pleasure in knowing poems by heart and learn them easily if they hear them often. Poetry is a natural extension of nursery rhyme. Lilt and rhythm are instinctive to childhood and can be enhanced, given form and expression, by familiarity with a wide range of poetry.

What shall I call
    My dear little dormouse?
His eyes are small,
    But his tail is e-nor-mouse.

(*A. A. Milne*)

Some one came knocking
    At my wee small door;
Some one came knocking,
    I'm sure—sure—sure . . .

(*Walter de la Mare*)

> Little wind, blow in the hill-top
> Little wind, blow on the plain
> Little wind, blow up the sunshine
> Little wind, blow off the rain
>
> *(Eleanor Farjeon)*

Wonder enters and stays with such poetry stored in the memory.

One of my children (the first Anthony) was fascinated when he was four by Robert Louis Stevenson's poem "Where Go the Boats?" (Even the title stirs the spirit!)

> Dark brown is the river,
> Golden is the sand,
> It flows along forever,
> With trees on either hand.
>
> Green leaves a-floating
> Castles of the foam,
> Boats of mine a-boating—
> Where will all come home?

This poem was Anthony's favorite for years. He was obviously carried away on the tide of the image it evoked for him.

> Away down the river,
> A hundred miles or more,
> Other little children
> Shall bring my boats ashore.

Hardly surprising that sailing later became one of this child's passions. I like to think that his love of the sea (and of books!) had its start in these long-ago reading sessions.

Don't neglect to point out to your child how different on the page different poems *look*. A familiar poem leaps at you from the page like an old friend. Long before he can read, your youngster will recognize the *shape* of a poem he loves, even in **an** unillustrated collection.

> John had
> Great Big
> Waterproof
> Boots on;
> John had a
> Great big
> Waterproof
> Hat;
> John had a
> Great Big
> Waterproof
> Mackintosh—
> And that
> (Said John)
> Is
> That.

A. A. Milne's poem, with its sturdy, stomping rhythm, sounds good, even without the book. But with the book—and an adult who will point to the words as they are said—the whole thing becomes a visual experience, as well as a listening treat.

Familiarity breeds affection in this field. Years ago in an old, much-loved volume, we had a copy of Rachel Field's "General Store."

> Some day I'm going to have a store
> With a tinkly bell hung over the door,
> With real glass cases and counters wide
> And drawers all spilly with things inside . . .

Somehow, we contrived to lose this anthology. When one of the family mentioned the poem later, I said, "Between us, we *must* know it by heart," and we found that we did. But it was not the same. We needed to *see* it, its solid, all-of-a-piece bulk sitting on the left side of the detailed, black-and-white line picture.

> It will be my store and I will say:
> What can I do for you today?

Met again, in a new collection several years later, it was greeted with cries of joyful recognition. Here was an old friend; but a slightly changed, because displaced, friend. The old, lost copy was never supplanted in our hearts.

It is advisable to read poetry alone, rehearsing its rhythms and absorbing its sense, before offering it to the young. There is nothing more enjoyable than reading aloud material that you know and love yourself, and this is particularly true of poetry. The child's enjoyment will reflect yours (a well-known phenomenon in any sphere); and enjoyment that is mutual is the most intense enjoyment of all.

Cynthia Mitchell has also written a collection of rhymes for the playground, which, with Eileen Browne's illustrations, are a joyful experience. It is called *Hop-Along Happily*, and its title poem (said to consist of thirty-one hops) goes:

> Hop-Along Happily
> Hopped through the wood
> Stopped by the toad's pond
> Slipped in the mud.
> Dripped through the shadows,
> Skipped up the path,
> Nipped up the back steps
> And hopped in the bath.

You can follow Hop-Along's progress from right to left round the double-page spread; from cheerful outset, through mishap to ultimate comfort (the last picture has him visible through the window, blissfully recumbent in a hot bath). This could be an ideal place to start, if you need to prove to yourself that you can include poetry in your read-aloud repertoire with success. The poems in this collection are all energetic, even jaunty, but they are diverse and original too.

The Young Puffin Book of Verse should be in every child's home, with another copy in the family car for emergencies. This paperback collection contains an astonishing number of the best poems ever written for children of four to eight—including "Some day I'm going to have a store . . ." On no account face life without it!

And on the family shelves, ready for instant and constant use, I can suggest nothing better than Louis Untermeyer's *Golden Treasury of Poetry.* This big, handsome book will serve any family of children faithfully and long. Its range is truly wide, and its aspect so friendly and well designed that even a small child will browse through it happily. Joan Walsh Anglund has found, here, the opportunity to produce illustrations of variety and imagination, and she has succeeded, triumphantly. Acquiring such a collection, so that you can use appropriate poems as the children grow into them has a lot to commend it and will also allow you to experiment. You may well be surprised at what your child has grown into while your back has been turned!

An anthology with a rather unusual bonus factor proved an excellent present for a five-year-old grandchild recently. *Fives, Sixes and Sevens* includes work of a number of famous poets— Eleanor Farjeon, Spike Milligan, James Reeves and Walter de la Mare are all represented—and yet achieves a fresh, original look. This springs from a combination of factors—excellent choice of simple but expressive poetry, the use of two-color line illustrations, and the choice of exceptionally large and clear print. This allows the child, once he knows the poems half by heart, to read them aloud, identifying the words as they spring to his lips. This is an excellent aid to learning to read, and a much underused technique, despite its accordance with modern findings about the reading process.

Edward Lear is a name you will come to know if you prove to enjoy reading poetry to your children (and you will, once you start!). Writing in the second half of the last century, Lear produced nonsense verse that has never been surpassed. You may have tried "A Was Once an Apple Pie" (Chapter 3) and *The Owl and the Pussycat* (Book List 1) already. Now it is time for more. Over-fours with their robust sense of fun and almost physical enjoyment of lilt and rhyme will love the simultaneous sobriety and absurdity of Lear's work.

You may well feel, if you are meeting Lear for the first time, that his poetry is too difficult for this age group. Many children, certainly, will not be ready for it until closer to six than four—but do try *The Jumblies* at least, after introducing the available picture-book poems. *The Jumblies* combines the advantages of a straightforward (however ridiculous) plot with vigorous yet simple language. For good measure, it has a catchy inter-verse chorus:

> Far and few, far and few
> Are the lands were the Jumblies live;
> Their heads are green and their hands are blue,
> And they went to sea in a Sieve.

There are a number of editions of Lear available, including collections which have the original illustrations by the poet himself. Two companion volumes, *The Jumblies and Other Nonsense Verses* and *The Pelican Chorus and Other Nonsense*

Verses, between them contain the best poems for reading aloud to young children, and these are my choice. Each is illustrated by Leslie Brooke, whose black-and-white illustrations are agreeable and meticulously detailed. Each title also has a number of colored plates or full-page inserted illustrations. Their slightly old-fashioned look is at one with Lear's precise, intricate and yet simple language and earnest yet lunatic stories. Try them out in private; you'll master the essential lilt quite quickly with a little practice—to your own and your youngster's very real pleasure.

I have spent what may seem to be a disproportionate time on poetry at the expense of stories and non-fiction for this age group. This is because I feel strongly about the child's need to experience language that is vital, resourceful, exhilarating, and harmonious, language that provides the human ear with a pointed and precise pleasure, which is not available from any other source, language that is crucial to the development of intelligence and self-expression.

Our society is becoming increasingly dependent on the visual image. Television selects what we will look at; advertisements are designed so that non-readers will still get the point. Sound is often loud, strident and undifferentiated. The precise, searching, illuminating impact of good and true words is in danger of being lost against the blaring and glaring background of the modern child's world. Parents are not to blame for this, and many of them, through no fault of their own, have no real feeling for the sort of language that will help their children to develop into sensitive, confident, articulate women and men. I believe that the best books, from birth, will do as much for parents as for children in this area, and at the same time keep them in touch with one another. And this is the most important thing of all.

I can hear readers asking all sorts of questions: What about sexism in children's books? Shouldn't we reject all books that show girls pursuing traditional girls' roles, boys doing all the exciting, extending things? Thousands of successful parents through the ages have taken no such drastic precautions, and have, nonetheless, raised vigorous, independent and self-accepting daughters—and sons. If books are good books, they engender true thoughts and feeling and so allow children to think clearly, to feel deeply. These children will make necessary changes in their own lives and, ultimately, in the wider world. Of course, we should reject those books that subtly and insidiously convey stereotyped attitudes; but these books are likely to be poor books in any case.

The best books reflect the best thought of their times. I believe that the best modern books will help us to raise children whose minds are free of unworthy prejudice, children who can love, and laugh, and get on with the business of living. I believe also that the best modern authors are conscious of the need to avoid stereotyping; that the campaigns which concerned people have conducted over the last decade or so, have borne fruit, and that we have, already, a growing body of good books that reflect their influence.

Five rising six is a good age; calmer and more assured than the year before, with less need for aggressive assertion, greater capacity for realistic self-assessment. The here-and-now satisfies this age group. Its members, attempting in the main only what is possible, are inclined to achieve, in a steady if unspectacular way. Troublesome times may lie ahead as horizons, beyond six, roll back and back. For the time being, the world is controllable because confined; success is achievable, problems surmountable.

The fortunate nearly-six-year-old uses language that is rich and resourceful to explain himself to others, to meet his own needs and to find out about his environment. His imagination is active, his sense of humor at the ready for laughter, his sympathy available, his love overflowing. Language, laughter, and love is the prescription; and each of these will have been fed, constantly and surely, by his contact with books, and with adults who have cared for him and have been prepared to use all the means at their disposal to help him to see the world squarely, to use its resources wisely. With conviction, and with good reason, the six-year-old announces:

> But now I am Six I'm as clever as clever,
> So I think I'll be Six now, for ever and ever.

Books to Use between Four and Six

The range of books available for this age group is very wide indeed, and care is necessary in selection.

I have personally used all the books listed with young children, and found them successful. (You can tell, from my comments, which ones brought down the house!)

For ease of reference, there are four special categories at the end of the list: Books for Special Situations, Collections of Stories, Poetry Books and Traditional Stories.

Enjoy them all!

(GB) *Angelo* Quentin Blake (Cape/Puffin paperback)
Angelo belongs to a long-ago family of wandering players; a happy family who enjoy their art and their way of life. Angelina, by contrast, lives with an old, mean, rich uncle, is badly treated and quite unloved. Her deliverance is portrayed energetically by both text and picture, against an authentic Old Italian background. A warm, humorous book.

● *A Baby Sister for Frances* Russell Hoban, illus. Lillian Hoban (Harper & Row)

● *Bedtime for Frances* Russell Hoban, illus. Lillian Hoban (Harper & Row)

(GB) *The Big Book of Machines*, in Color: (Collins)
This book reveals to the fascinated gaze of the "big machine" addict, a galaxy of monsters: drag-line machines, excavators, bulldozers, combine harvesters, hovercraft—even a Moon Rover. The text is for adults, though the well-read four-year-old will relish the technicalities—and the less "verbal" love the accurate, large-as-life pictures.

(GB) *The Big Snowstorm*   Hans Peterson, illus. Harald Wiberg   (Burke)

This book is almost a documentary. It concerns the activities, fears and excitements of life in an isolated Swedish farmhouse in the depths of winter. A peddler is rescued and given shelter, a calf is born, a small boy learns that he can do his share in an emergency. Harald Wiberg's illustrations create an atmosphere at once mysterious and homely. The beauty and starkness of the Northern winter is portrayed in both text and picture.

The Boy Who Was Followed Home   Margaret Mahy, illus. Steven Kellogg   (Watts)

Robert is an ordinary little boy to whom an extraordinary thing happens; first one, then two, and ultimately forty-three hippopotami follow him home from school. The pictures make no attempt to be funny; they merely illustrate the text and are detailed, earnest and hilarious. All is well, in the end, Robert thinks . . . (How wrong he is is revealed on the last page). A great joy, this book.

● (GB) *A Brother for Momoko*   Chihiro Iwasaki   (Bodley Head)

The Bunyip of Berkeley's Creek   Jenny Wagner, illus. Ron Brooks   (Bradbury Press/Penguin paperback)

The legendary Bunyip of Australia here takes form and sets out to discover his identity. The gentle creature suffers successive rebuffs before—joy of joys!—*another* bunyip arises "from the black mud at the bottom of the billabong" to join him. The illustrations reveal craftsmanship of a high order. They are unusual, unearthly and eloquent. An outstanding book.

Burglar Bill   Janet and Allan Ahlberg   (Greenwillow/Penguin paperback)

A rousing story of a cheerful, warm-hearted burglar who steals a "nice big brown box with little holes in it." When it proves to contain a baby, Bill is in a quandary—until he is burgled by Burglar Betty who is, of course, the baby's mother. A rollicking romp of a book with considerable text—but such fun that the average five-year-old will love it. The pictures strike exactly the right note—and Betty and Bill marry, reform and return all their joint loot. (Crime must, of course, be seen not to pay!)

● *The Carrot Seed* Ruth Krauss, illus. Crockett Johnson   (Harper & Row/Scholastic paperback)

● *Christmas in the Stable*   Astrid Lindgren, illus. Harald Wiberg   (Coward, McCann & Geoghegan)

Could Be Worse! James Stevenson   (Greenwillow/Penguin paperback)
This hilarious story will appeal to the reckless in the over-fours. Mary Ann and Louie think that Grandpa is very dull (and he is) until one morning he explodes into a breathtaking, pell-mell account of what happened to him during the night. An astonishing catalogue of unlikely near-catastrophes will keep eyes popping and mouths gaping. The pictures take off in wild comic-book gallop, which captures the spirit exactly.

The Country Bunny and the Little Gold Shoes DuBose Heyward, illus. Marjorie Flack   (Houghton Mifflin)
An old book (1956) of singular, inexplicable appeal to the young. Little Mother Cottontail has all the (out-dated) domestic virtues; her children are numerous, greatly loved, carefully trained, and well disciplined. Motherhood, however, does not prevent her from applying for a top position among the Easter Bunnies when one falls vacant and actually aids and abets her in her victory over her male contestants. (Those of us who believe that women can enjoy two roles simultaneously, and are inordinately privileged in this respect, will rejoice to see her, victorious and fulfilled on both fronts!) The young, who care nothing for these considerations, will be engrossed by the considerable but clear text and detailed illustrations. This is *the* Easter book, in my opinion!

● *Crocodile Medicine* Marjorie-Ann Watts   (Warne)

(GB) *Diana and Her Rhinoceros* Edward Ardizzone   (Bodley Head)

A story at once credible and unbelievable; sensible and absurd; stately and undignified; hilariously funny and deeply serious. Only Ardizzone can do this, and he brings it off to perfection here. Diana has good sense, resourcefulness and serenity. (The Victorians might have seen her as an Example. Feminists will certainly claim her as a Sister.) An enduring book.

● (GB) *Dogger* Shirley Hughes (Bodley Head)

● (GB) *Don't Forget, Matilda* Ronda and David Armitage (Deutsch)

(GB) *The Dragon of an Ordinary Family* Margaret Mahy, illus. Helen Oxenbury (Heinemann)
A rollicking yarn about the acquisition by an ordinary family of a pet dragon. An engrossing experience, for which the illustrations must be held half responsible.

Fourteen Rats and a Rat-Catcher Tamasin Cole (Prentice-Hall)
An exercise in viewpoints: upstairs, a nice old lady plans to rid her house of the nasty rats in the cellar. In the cellar, a nice rat family would be happy, were it not for the nasty old lady living above them . . . The illustrations, framed in chocolate-brown borders (with the text similary framed below) are outstanding. Rich color and excellent design combine with a funny, tongue-in-cheek tale to create an assuredly successful book.

Grandfather Jeannie Baker (Deutsch)
A picture book of feeling, rather than happening. The little girl's grandfather keeps a junk shop. By way of the artist's fascinating, meticulously engineered collages, we are enabled to share the wonder and the diversity of the shop's contents through the child's eyes. A book for long-looking and endless finding.

(GB) *Gumdrop* Val Biro (Hodder & Stoughton/Piccolo paperback)
Gumdrop is a real car, who belongs to the author. He is an Austin Clifton Twelve-Four and was made in 1926. (There are enchant-

ing diagrams of his innards on the endpapers.) Within the book he is given colorful life and real style by Val Biro's jaunty, bright and copious illustrations. Gumdrop has a capacity for trouble that is irresistible; and if you like him, there are at least eight titles.

George the Babysitter   Shirley Hughes   (Prentice-Hall)
George is a teenage babysitter; clearly known and loved by Mick, Jenny and the baby, Sue, clearly determined to cope, and just as clearly defeated by the children's children-ness and the consequent impossibility of changing anything or reforming anyone. He and they are warm, accepting, loving—and natural. As is Mum, when she returns. George is exhausted . . . but cheerful still. Shirley Hughes creates children who live, breathe, exasperate and delight. A joy of a book.

● *Happy Birthday, Sam*   Pat Hutchins   (Greenwillow)
An Invitation to the Butterfly Ball   Jane Yolen, illus. Jane Breskin Zelben   (Parents Magazine Press)

> Knock. Knock. Who's come to call?
> An invitation to the Butterfly Ball.

One little mouse, two little moles, three little rabbits . . . up to ten little porcupines, all are invited to the Butterfly Ball. All have problems equipping themselves suitably for the great event, but none is as desperate as the little mouse who

> looks all over for a floor-length dress.
> If she can't find one smaller than small,
> Then she can't go to the Butterfly Ball.

Success on all fronts is gloriously celebrated on the last double-spread page. This is a counting book for fives and sixes; the language is well-tuned and simple, but the text longer than usual. The illustrations are exquisitely delicate, faithful to the text, and beautiful.

John Brown, Rose and the Midnight Cat Jenny Wagner, illus.
Ron Brooks (Bradbury Press/Penguin paperback)
Domestic devotion between John Brown, a gloriously huge and
shaggy dog, and Rose, whose "husband died a long time ago," is
undisturbed until "the midnight cat" appears in the garden. Rose
wants to take him in; John Brown is obstructive. The illustrations
are striking; soft, night-time colors reflect the mood faithfully.
The domestic interior is scrupulously detailed, the outdoor
scenes authentic to the missing fence post. An unusual, important
book with an unobstructive but certain message.

Katy No Pocket Emmy Payne, illus. H. A. Rey (Houghton
Mifflin)
This book starts as a rather trite, contrived affair and ends as a triumph of love and determination. Katy Kangaroo has, alas, no
pocket in which to carry Freddy, her baby kangaroo. She con-
sults respected authorities—and the owl sends her to the city
where, he says "... they sell that sort of thing ..."
From here on, it is inspired. Katy returns from the city en-
cased in a carpenter's apron, in the pockets of which there is
room, not only for Freddy but for a dozen or so more baby animals (of a *very* diverse sort!) Katy is a creature of expansive love
and simple generosity. The whole thing is simultaneously cheap-
looking and infinitely precious, in the real sense of the word.
(Our copy has "Josephine Butler, May 1965" written in the
front. Jo would have been five, and very bookwise; but Katy, for
comfort, was indispensable.)

The Lady Who Saw the Good Side of Everything Pat Decker
Tapio, illus. Paul Galdone (Seabury)
Indomitable optimism in the person of a sprightly old lady who
survives catastrophe after cataclysm (her house is washed away
by a flood, and she remarks brightly: "I needed a new house anyway."). Funny, and yet sound, too—and Paul Galdone's wide-
page, full-color illustrations catch the mood precisely.

● (GB) *The Lighthouse Keeper's Lunch*　Ronda and David Armitage　(Deutsch)

● *Little Bear*　Else Holmelund Minarik, illus. Maurice Sendak　(Harper & Row)

● *The Little Boy and His House*　Stephen Bone and Mary Adshead　(Dent)

● *The Little Boys and Their Boats*　Stephen Bone and Mary Adshead　(Dent)

(GB) *The Little Car Has a Day Out*　Leila Berg and Leslie Wood　(Hodder & Stoughton)

The little car and his driver have a happy and interesting day in the country. Brightly colored illustrations provide a wealth of viewing detail, and the text is lively.

(GB) *The Little Girl and The Tiny Doll*　Edward & Aingelda Ardizzone　(Kestrel)

An exceptional book, which defies description. Enough to say that it has a proven capacity to fascinate that transcends its modest appearance; a singular quality that ensures rapt attention from the first page. A tiny doll is dropped into the deep-freeze in a grocer's shop by a child who "did not care for dolls." The doll is seen by another child, who undertakes her care at long range. Ardizzone's eye and ear for the concerns of the young are impeccable. Here is perfect pitch and true vision.

● *The Little Gorilla*　Ruth Bornstein　(Seabury)

The Little House　Virginia Lee Burton　(Houghton Mifflin)

Mike Mulligan and His Steam Shovel　Virginia Lee Burton　(Houghton Mifflin)

It's impossible to think of these two superlative products of this century's picture-book art, except together (they were both first published in the early forties).

　　The first tells the story of a humble little house, which began her life "... on a little hill, covered with daisies and apple trees growing around . . ." Through endless days, nights, seasons and years, the little house stays the same. But the countryside does not; gradually the landscape is transformed, as first roads, then buildings, then a subway, then an overhead railway, surround and ultimately swamp her. Her deliverance is triumphant; she is discovered by "the great-great-granddaughter of the man who built the house so well. . . ," and towed away, ". . . to a little hill, covered in daisies." The detail is copious and meticulous, the whole a joy.

Mike Mulligan and his steam shovel, Mary-Ann, win all hearts, on acquaintance. Mike cannot bear to discard Mary-Ann, despite her outdated and outworn condition. In the end, he doesn't have to. The story has tension, climax, warmth and imagination; its message concerns the capacity of goodness and courage to convert spite and greed to its own ranks. Young children ought not to miss it; the illustrations support and extend its impact.

(GB) *The Little Old Man Who Could Not Read*   Irma Simonton Black, illus. Seymour Fleishman   (World's Work)
One might not approve, if this story demonstrated only the inadvisability of not learning to read! As it is, it is humorous, human and heart-warming. The little man has never before wanted to learn to read, and never needed to; but when his wife goes on holiday and he has to do the shopping . . . The pictures support and extend the jaunty text. Propaganda without preaching.

Little Owl   Reiner Zimnik and Hanne Axmann (Atheneum)
A lengthy, absorbing story which will appeal to five-year-olds, and good listeners among the fours. Zimnik writes superbly, and the illustrations in bold primary color complement the story splendidly. The little owl is fascinated by the people who live in the big house opposite the park, but only little Klaus is friendly; and Clothilde, the washerwoman, is frightened of him. Then, one night, there is a fire, and Little Owl becomes a hero.

(GB) *The Little Shunting Engine*   Ib Spang Olsen   (World's Work)

There is a literary tradition of rebellious trains leaping off the rails, but the little shunting engine is in a class of its own. This engine is accidentally started, and only begins doing unconventional things when it runs out of line. The black-and-white illustrations, enlivened with touches of red, green and brown, are satisfyingly in tune with the story, which is exciting and funny—and not too alarming.

Little Tim and the Brave Sea Captain   Edward Ardizzone   (Oxford University Press)

This author-artist's work is superlative; it has no counterpart, though many adults cannot understand its success with the young. Suffice to say that Tim, the boy hero, while prey to all the human frailties and trials (fear, homesickness, despair,—even seasickness!) is throughout steadfast, courageous, loyal and *ordinary*. Ardizzone has never lost a degree of childlike ingenuousness; and he understands a child's need to see himself as the adults' equal. These are believable if outrageous stories of children behaving as adults. They have warmth, vigor, the assurance of coming home in the end, and the conviction that home, family and friends matter most of all. There are eleven "Little Tim" books. Just as good is *Nicholas and the Fast Moving Diesel* and, in a different but recognizably Ardizzone way, *Lucy Brown and Mr Grimes* (Bodley Head).

● (GB) *Long Ago in Bethlehem*   Masahiro Kasuya   (A. & C. Black)

(GB) *Lotta's Bike*   Astrid Lindgren, illus. Ilon Wikland   (Methuen)

Lotta is five, and rather big for her boots. It's her birthday, and she had wanted a bike more than anything else. After all, her big brother and sister, Jonas and Maria, both have bikes . . . Her solution is in character and almost, but not quite, wrecks the big·

day. The pictures in this slice-of-life book have cosiness and color and just avoid sentimentality. Instead, they achieve a sort of homely virtuosity that is irresistible.

● *Madeline*   Ludwig Bemelmans   (Viking Press/Penguin paperback)

● (GB) *Maisie Middleton*   Nina Sowter   (A. & C. Black)

Make Hay While the Sun Shines: A Book of Proverbs   Chosen by Alison M. Abel illus. Shirley Hughes   (Faber)
A unique book. How many modern children hear the old proverbs used, as did an earlier generation? (Memory, being stirred up, comes up with a warm feeling for a father who used to say, "It's no use crying over spilt milk . . .") Shirley Hughes's cheerfully scruffy modern children and adults gazing into shop windows ("All that glitters is not gold"), scrubbing floors ("Many hands make light work"), and landing in unsuspected ponds ("Look before you leap") present modern children with the comfort and security of an older age—and bolster their "language" repertoire.

Mouse Trouble   John Yeoman, illus. Quentin Blake   (Macmillan)
A miserly miller beset with mice, and a cat who can't cope and whose cause is espoused by the mice, ensure hilarity and improbability in equal proportions. The rollicking tale is further enlivened by illustrations of virtuosity. One almost feels sorry for the miller!

● *Moving Molly*   Shirley Hughes   (Prentice-Hall)

(GB) *My Grandpa Is a Pirate*   Jan Loof   (A. & C. Black)
A deadpan description of an adventure undertaken by a small boy and his grandfather, a pirate ("He's making it all up!" says Grandma. "He has worked in the post office all his life.") It has everything: buried treasure, a map, cannons, cutlasses—all amassed in impressive, clear, double-spread pictures. (Fortu-

nately, Grandma stays asleep long enough for them to escape, and make it home.) People of five—and fifty—love it.

My Little Hen   Alice and Martin Provensen   (Random House)
This is a small gem of a book, apparently simple enough for under-fours. It has undertones however—and is so delicately beautiful, with its Victorian photo-album format, that I would keep it for the five-year-old. It's about Emily's hen Etta, her dog Ralph, her cat Max, Etta's chicken Neddy (later Netta, for obvious reasons) and their developing relationships. The whole book has a rare, exquisite quality—and the final picture, of all Etta and Netta's "children and the children's children" is utterly enchanting.

Natasha's New Doll   Frank Francis   (O'Hara)
What starts as a cosy domestic story of a small Russian peasant girl receiving a new (very old) doll turns into high drama when Natasha, going to meet her father, entangles with a witch in the forests. But Anna, the doll, proves to be more than she appears ... The pace is lively and the illustrations striking in this successful book.

The Nickle Nackle Tree   Lynley Dodd   (Macmillan)
An unusual counting book in which original and spirited verse is complemented by elegant and sprightly pictures.

> Seven haughty Huffpuff birds with hoity-toity smiles
> Eight cheeky Chizzle birds in cheerful chirpy piles

The ultimate collapse of the overloaded Nickle Nackle Tree is predictable and amusing.

The Nutshell Library   Maurice Sendak   (Harper & Row)
Four enchanting little books in a slipcase. All children love miniature objects, and these tiny volumes are splendid books in their own right. There is a counting book, a cautionary tale, an alpha-

bet and a book of months and seasons—all distinguished by Sendak's singular and pointed use of words, and his incomparably earthly, knowing illustrations.

(GB) *Oliver Ostrich*   Sheila Lavelle, illus. Nina Sowter   (A. & C. Black)

A hilarious romp of a book. Oliver belongs to the long-suffering Button family, whose possessions he is steadily consuming. The resolution is brilliant—and so are the bold, earthy, colorful pictures.

(GB) *On My Way to School*   Celia Berridge   (Deutsch)

"This is the house that I leave each day on my way to school," begins this accomplished little story. In brilliantly colored, clear but detailed illustrations it takes a small girl to school, sees her through the day in two textless double spreads, and then takes her home. The repetition is not overdone and the simple sentences have energy rather than sobriety. Beginning readers will profit from the very clearly produced print under each picture.

● *Phoebe and the Hot Water Bottles*   Terry Furchgott and Linda Dawson   (Deutsch)

(GB) *The Penguin and the Vacuum Cleaner*   Carolyn Sloan, illus. Jill McDonald   (Kestrel/Puffin paperback)

Four- to six-year-olds domestic chaos, and the mess made by the penguin and his "friend" the vacuum cleaner is prodigious! Josh has fed the cleaner ". . . all the feathers out of his pillow, some flour and a tin of sardines . . ." (and much more) before it finally ". . . gave a hiccup and blew out a green flash." The illustrations are in brilliant color, the text jaunty and straightforward in this original book.

Potter Brownware   Sarah Garland   (Scribner)

Rather specialized, perhaps (and all very well for my family; two of my grandchildren have a potter for a father, and a house and garden just like the Brownwares's!). But why not learn about different lifestyles early? The Brownware family are loving and robust, their story a triumphant one. The text is simple, well-positioned and clear, the illustrations vigorous and colorful (with a totally appropriate brown-ness).

The Rain Puddle Adelaide Holl, illus. Roger Duvoisin (Lothrop, Lee & Shepard)
An apparently simple story; but one that requires an understanding of reflections, and the way they work. A farmyard hen decides that another hen has fallen into a large rain puddle. All the other animals come to see for themselves, and draw predictable conclusions. The action is portrayed clearly, in pictures of pleasing design and robust color. The animal noises ("Gobble-obble-obble! Snort, snort! Oink, oink!") are certain to delight, even if the point is missed at first.

The Sign on Rosie's Door Maurice Sendak (Harper & Row)
There are four separate stories about the same group of children in this baffling book (Sendak bypasses adults when addressing children, which he likes most to do). You may think there is no child quite as strange as yours until you meet Rosie, Kathy, Lenny, Pudgy, Sal and Dolly. You will then recognize the uniqueness and the sameness of all children everywhere. This is probably the only book ever written that should be issued by "the authorities" to all the five-year-olds in the world. You can't afford to let yours miss it.

(GB) *Snail and Caterpillar* Helen Piers, illus. Pauline Baynes (Kestrel)
Grasshopper and Butterfly Helen Piers, illus. Pauline Baynes (McGraw-Hill)
Detailed stories of small creatures of the countryside, brought to life by Pauline Baynes's exquisite illustrations. Considerable information is effortlessly absorbed, but the books are more than mere nature lessons.

The Story About Ping Majorie Flack and Kurt Wiese (Viking Press/Penguin paperback)

Ping is a duck of originality. His home is a boat on the Yangtse River to which he must return each night. But one night, he rebels. His subsequent adventures have become justly famous since his emergence in 1935. Text and pictures are well integrated in this sound and satisfying book.

● *The Story of Christmas* Felix Hoffman (Atheneum)

The Story of Ferdinand Munro Leaf, illus. Robert Lawson (Viking Press/Penguin paperback)

First published in 1937, the tale of Ferdinand, the gentle bull who triumphs in the face of aggression, goes from strength to strength. The black-and-white illustrations evoke Spain, bull-fights, and the impossibility of violence when one of the parties simply won't cooperate. "So they had to take Ferdinand home ..."

A classic, which may be overlooked unless especially sought out.

(GB) *The Story of Horace* Alice M. Coates (Faber/Faber paperback)

The sophisticated humor of this classic tale (first published in 1937) is within reach of the advanced five- to six-year-old by reason of its riotous, slapstick humor. Horace, a bear unwisely kept by a human family, gradually eats them all: Great-Grandpa, Great-Grandma, Grandpa, Grandma, Pa, Ma, Paul and Little Lulu. Father returning each night, threatens ". . . to *kill* Horace!" This sensible precaution keeps being deferred, because ". . . they all took on so, he hadn't the heart to do it"!

The end is self-huggingly predictable. The pictures are modest, representational, almost diagrammatic. The whole constitutes a work of real virtuosity. (Read it to your youngster with gusto and amusement, and his reception will echo yours.)

The Summer Night Charlotte Zolotow, illus. Ben Shecter (Harper & Row)

A gentle, absorbing story about a father who cares for his little girl, and how they spend an evening together when she cannot sleep. Their relationship is sympathetically evoked by the quiet, descriptive text and the sensitive, somberly peaceful pictures of the night, indoors and out. A true bedtime story—but its calm, dreamlike quality could be useful at any hour.

Sven's Bridge   Anita Lobel   (Harper & Row)
Sven tends his drawbridge with care, until it is destroyed through the king's anger and impatience. So he builds a ferry . . . The outcome, when the king's carriage crashes into the river, is as happy as it is unforeseen. Sound, implicit moral, and enchantingly detailed, bordered illustrations together cater for practical as well as literary over-fours.

Tell Me a Mitzi   Lore Segal, illus. Harriet Pincus   (Farrar, Straus & Giroux)
Three picture books in one; each about Mitzi, her parents, and her baby brother Jacob. Each has individuality and style, but the first, *Mitzi Takes a Taxi*, is unmatched in picture books for a quality that transfixes children while it exasperates adults; its sheer, unbelievably meticulous, outrageously unnecessary, repetitious and *endless* description of what is going on.

> . . . So Mitzi got Jacob's bottle, carried it into the
> kitchen and opened the refrigerator and took
> out a carton of milk and opened it and took the
> top off Jacob's bottle and poured in the milk
> and put the top back on and closed the carton
> and put it back in the refrigerator and closed
> the door and carried the bottle into the
> children's room and gave it to Jacob and said,
> "Let's go."

The illustrations are so right that one can only assume author and artist to be totally in tune. A signal book.

The Terrible Tiger Jack Prelutsky, illus. Arnold Lobel (Macmillan)
This is an unusually wordy picture book, which is invariably popular with fives and sixes. The tiger is ferocious and immodest: "Yes, I'm the most terrible, terrible, terrible tiger that ever has been."

He is outwitted by his victims, in the end, but not humbled. Children like his cheek, his arrogance, his sheer guts!

The Tiger-Skin Rug Gerald Rose   (Prentice-Hall)
A truly hilarious story about a dusty, moth-eaten old tiger who manages to pass himself off as a rug in the Rajah's palace. Highly original theme, well-rounded plot and lively, colorful pictures ensure its success with small readers and their parents. He's a *character*, this particular tiger!

Tilly's House Faith Jaques   (Atheneum)
An outstanding picture book on a subject that has perennial appeal for the over-fours. House-or-hut building really enter the scene at this stage; and the appeal of dolls' houses is ageless. Tilly is an oppressed but spirited little kitchenmaid in a Victorian dolls' house, until her moment of rebellion arrives. A decision to find "a place where I can be free and decide things for myself" launches her into an escape, which is documented in detail in the meticulous and charming pictures. The home that Tilly subsequently sets up in the garden shed is evidence of her incomparable ingenuity, resourcefulness and industry. Teddy helps, but is bumbling by comparison. Tilly's achievements are direct reflections of her cosy maxims:

> Where there's a will there's a way.
> Waste not, want not!

A joy for all children lucky enough to meet it.

Tom Fox and the Apple Pie Clyde Watson, illus. Wendy Watson   (T. Y. Crowell)

Tom was the youngest of the little foxes and certainly the laziest and greediest. His story is told in spirited but simple language and brought alive by exceptional, woodcut-like illustrations in black, white and turquoise. The theme is both funny and very human (Tom *means* to keep some of the pie for his sisters and brothers, but . . .) Children will understand!

(GB) *The Toymaker's Loaves*   Jennifer Zabel and Christopher Masters   (Warne)
The story of Mr. Tinkerman, who made carved wooden toys, and how he was obliged to become a baker instead. This didn't pay either, until he hit upon the idea of combining his two arts, and producing "fat little teddy bears, chubby dolls, marvellous motor cars and beaming golliwogs, all with the golden crustiness of fresh bread." Success at last! The humorous, lively illustrations have as much to say to the youngster as the words.

(GB) *The Trouble with Jack*   Shirley Hughes   (Bodley Head/Lion paperback)
This engaging story is simple enough for a younger child—but the message is for a big sister. Jack (about two) almost wrecks Nancy's party, but, after the crisis is resolved, she reflects: "The trouble with Jack . . . is that as he's my brother I've got to put up with him whatever he's like." Shirley Hughes's children are, as usual, flesh and blood.

(GB) *The Truck on the Track*   Janet Burroway, illus. John Vernon Lord   (Cape/Piccolo paperback)
A mad saga of unrewarded effort. The Barney Bros. Circus truck is stuck on the railway track. All efforts to move it (both sensible and bizarre) prove fruitless. "The truck still stuck." In the end, the feckless band set up camp and wait for the train to come. "Whack! Tough luck." The picture of tangled truck and train is indescribable, and so is child reception of this extraordinary book. To miss it at the right age is to be deprived.

(GB) *Varenka*   Bernadette Watts   (Oxford)
Varenka lived long ago in a little house in one of the great forests
of Russia. When war was being waged nearby, she did not flee;
she must stay to look after travellers, lost children and animals.
Her prayer that God would build a high wall round her little
house was answered in a way she could not foresee. The illustrations have a formal, glowing beauty, and are yet, like the story,
full of feeling.

The Web in the Grass   Berniece Freschet, illus. Roger Duvoisin   (Scribners)
An honest and yet compassionate view of the fierce world of the
small spider, who must spin ceaselessly if she is to catch food, create a padded sac for her eggs, and evade her many enemies. A fascinating view of a dangerous and beautiful world, brilliantly illustrated in color.

A Week Is a Long Time   Pat Barton, illus. Jutta Ash (Abelard-
Schuman)
Honey Brown is going to stay with Great Aunt Em in the country. Aunt Em, and Mrs. Biggs, who lives with her, are waiting for
Honey to arrive. They all reflect that "A week is a long time . . ."
In the event, it flies by. The two old ladies live in an old Victorian
house with "no toys" but "a dressing-up box." At the end of the
week Honey goes home to face a new baby brother, musing to
herself "How nice . . . that a week *is* such a long time."

The black-and-white illustrations demonstrate the suitability of this medium for the depiction of sensitive shades of meaning.

(GB) *What Do People Do All Day?*   Richard Scarry   (Collins)
They dig and cook and paint and drive and clean and build . . .
and in this very large, colorful volume you can watch them doing
it. Scarry's busy little animal-people provide fascinating enter-
tainment for the young, either to enjoy alone, or with obliging
adult on hand to help.

William the Dragon Polly Donnison (Coward, McCann & Geoghegan)
A dragon who hatches out in a stately home (on Lady Wilmount's bed, no less) and thereafter takes up residence in Lady W.'s heart as well as home is not to be ignored. He is, in the event, worth knowing in his own right ... and in the hardback version of his life story there are five carefully illustrated tales about him. A masterly accomplishment, this book. And was there ever a better-named vet than Mr. Horsepill?)

The Year at Maple Hill Farm Alice and Martin Provensen (Atheneum)
This book elicits a delighted gasp at first opening, long sighs of satisfaction thereafter. The more mass market big books look shoddy beside this testimony to the infinite art and singular skill that have together produced it. Detailed month-by-month vistas of farm life from January to January are supported by a text that gives just the right amount of information. Endless viewing is encouraged—impossible to resist, actually. No need for slick, overclever gimmickry. The Provensens are masters of their art, and their book reflects this mastery.

● *Curious George* by H. A. Rey (Houghton-Mifflin/Sandpaperback)

● *Curious George Goes to the Hospital* by H. A. Rey (Houghton-Mifflin)

BOOKS FOR SPECIAL SITUATIONS

A Baby in the Family Althea Braithwaite (Paul Elek)
A straightforward account of family life and reproduction. Sex differences are described and shown, intercourse explained, and birth presented both in text and illustration. The pictures are clear and colorful, and avoid sentimentality while achieving good taste.

How Babies are Made A. C. Andry and S. Schepp, illus. B. Hamptom (Time-Life)
Visually arresting, this book begins with the reproductive details of flowers and moves, by way of chickens and dogs, to human beings. It is honest, in no way coy or falsified, and its approach is simple and scientific. Intercourse is explained and birth shown in the clear, collage-style pictures used throughout the book.

● *Don't Foget Tom* Hanne Larsen (T Y Crowell)

● (GB) *Mr. Fairweather and His Family* Margaret Kornitzer, illus. Shirley Hughes (Bodley Head)

● (GB) *The Hollywell Family* Margaret Kornitzer, illus. Margery Gill (Bodley Head)

● *The Tenth Good Thing About Barney* Judith Viorst, illus. Erik Blegvad (Atheneum)

When Violet Died Mildred Kantrowitz, illus. Emily A. McCully (Parents)
Amy and Eva are upset when their bird, Violet, dies. The funeral, attended by Billy and Elizabeth from next door, is a sad occasion—but rather fun, too—and after all, their cat Blanche is about to have kittens. A sound, life-supporting picture book about death.

COLLECTIONS OF STORIES

The following books are all suitable for use in read-aloud sessions. Most have few illustrations and provide different experiences from picture-book viewing.

(GB) *Carrot Tops* Joan Wyatt (Hienemann/Puffin paperback)
Simple, realistic stories of everyday doings.

Milly-Molly-Mandy Joyce Lankester Brisley (McKay)
The small heroine and her family and friends have enchanted children for years, and continue to do so.

● (GB) *The Ruth Ainsworth Book* Ruth Ainsworth, illus. Shirley Hughes (Heinemann)

Stories for Five-Year-Olds and other young readers Sara & Stephen Corrin (Faber/Puffin paperback)
This and the following title provide a rich selection of stories.

Stories for Under-Fives Sara & Stephen Corrin (Faber/Puffin paperback)

(GB) *Tell Me A Story*

(GB) *Tell Me Another Story*

(GB) *Time for a Story* all by Eileen Colwell (Puffin paperback)
Three established paperback collections. The stories are all sound and usable. Keep an extra copy of your favorite in car or handbag.

● (GB) *To Read and to Tell* Norah Montgomerie, illus. Margery Gill (Bodley Head)

POETRY BOOKS

(GB) *The Dong with the Luminous Nose* and Other Poems, by Edward Lear, illus. Gerald Rose (Faber)
Picture-book format and spirited, vivid illustrations. Includes "The Jumblies," "The Owl and the Pussycat" and "The Duck and the Kangaroo"—which, with the title poem, make a good beginning with this author.

● (GB) *Fives Sixes and Sevens* Marjorie Stephenson, illus. Denis Wrigley (Warne)

● *The Golden Treasury of Poetry* (Louis Untermeyer, illus. Joan Walsh Anglund (Western Publishing Co.)

● *Halloweena Hecatee & Other Rhymes to Skip to Playground* Cynthia Mitchell, illus. Eileen Browne (T. Y. Crowell)

● *The Jumblies and Other Nonsense Verses* Edward Lear, illus. Leslie Brooke (Warne) and:

● *The Pelican Chorus and Other Nonsense Verses* Edward Lear, illus. Leslie Brooke (Warne)

(GB) *The Quangle Wangle's Hat* Edward Lear, pictures by Helen Oxenbury (Heinemann/Puffin paperback)
Probably (with "The Owl and the Pussycat") the best Lear of all to start with.

> On top of the Crumpetty Tree
> The Quangle Wangle sat,
> But his face you could not see,
> On account of his Beaver Hat.
> For his Hat was a hundred and two feet wide,
> With ribbons and bibbons on every side,
> And bells, and buttons, and loops, and lace,
> So that nobody ever could see the face
> Of the Quangle Wangle Quee.

The illustrations are magnificent; in conception, in color, in impact.

● *Playtime* Cynthia Mitchell, illus. Satomi Ichikawa (William Collins)

● (GB) *The Young Puffin Book of Verse* Barbara Ireson (Puffin paperback)

TRADITIONAL STORIES

The following editions will appeal to children between four and six. Many of them will endure for years, and will be enjoyed in new and more complex versions as time goes by. Stories and fables from famous collectors have been grouped together under appropriate headings at the end, with a brief note about each.

Chanticleer and the Fox Barbara Cooney (T. Y. Crowell)
It is never too soon for children to become accustomed to well-

tuned prose that has borrowed the flavor of its original, in this case the medieval earthiness and rhythm of Chaucer's *Canterbury Tales*. The story is stirring and Barbara Cooney's illustrations have a startling, glowing quality.

Noah's Ark Peter Spier (Doubleday)
A notable, medal-winning book which, after reproduction on the first page of an ancient, staccato poem relating Noah's story, confines itself to pictures. These are more than adequate to tell the story. This artist excels always at intricate detail and has here surpassed himself.

The Hobyahs Simon Stern (Prentice-Hall)
Impossible to capture in words the essence of this old story. The Hobyahs are squat, hideous mini-monsters, who are guaranteed to enchant while they horrify. Their determined persecution of "the old man, the old woman and the little girl," (averted in the end by Little Dog Turpie), is hair-raising in the event, but funny once over. This is a memorable story, encapsulated here in a tiny book. The small, framed, purply-brown pictures and hand-lettered text are just right.

The Little Hen and The Giant Maria Polushkin, illus. Yuri Salzman (Harper & Row/Scholastic Book Services paperback)
This simultaneously frightening and funny tale claims to have "the flavor of old Russia." It certainly has style, wild exaggeration and rough humor—as well as vigorous, individual illustrations, which catch the flavor exactly. Altogether a book that will impress, amuse and call for repetition.

Little Sister and the Month Brothers Beatrice Schenk de Regniers, illus. Margaret Tomes (Seabury)
Suitable for the upper age-level of this group—and how superbly suitable! This is a Slavic tale and is told with sensitivity and great skill, by a craftsman in the field. The illustrations have, miraculously, the same touch. This is masterly matching, the book a triumph of literary-artistic integration.

● *The Magic Porridge Pot* Paul Galdone (Seabury)

The Tomten Astrid Lindgren, illus. Harald Wiberg (Coward, McCann & Geoghegan)

A book of unique quality. This is the story of a small Swedish troll ". . . an old old Tomten who has seen the snow of many hundreds of winters . . ." who lives at an old farm, deep in the forest. No one has ever seen him, but each night he plods from animal to animal, comforting them, and talking to them in tomten language, "a silent little language a horse can understand." Each whole-page picture almost demands to be framed and hung. The mood of the long Northern night shines from these somber, glowing scenes; and the text is sheer poetry. To be a child is to wonder. How could this evocation of remote serenity *not* bolster and fortify?

> Winters come and summers go, year follows year,
>   but as long as people live at the old farm in the
>   forest, every night the Tomten will trip around
>   between the houses on his small silent feet.

The Fox and the Tomten by the same author, is recommended.

Why Noah chose the Dove Isaac Bashevis Singer, illus. Eric Carle (Farrar, Straus & Giroux)

All the animals compete for distinction in this repetitive story with a moral. But Noah chooses the dove, who ". . . remained modest and silent while the rest . . . bragged and argued . . ." Eric Carle's brilliantly colored, starkly stated pictures of animals and landscapes steal the show, at first contact. But the text has a measured elegance which carries weight, and brings home the message delicately but surely.

Hans Andersen was a Danish writer of fairy stories who lived in the nineteenth century. Many of his tales have an affinity with other European stories. Many are too long and complex for younger children, but the following stories will be enjoyed by four- and five-year-olds.

The Emperor's New Clothes   Jack Kent   (Four Winds Press)
(GB) *The Emperor's New Clothes*   Fulvio Testa   (Abelard-Schuman)
Two individual interpretations by very different artists. The humorous nature of the well-known story plays into Jack Kent's hands; his naked emperor is pink, chubby, and lovable. By contrast, Testa's illustrations have dignity and impressive design; but humor and radiant color, too. Children will profit from both, and the inevitable comparison will increase their awareness of different styles.

The Princess and the Pea   Paul Galdone   (Seabury)
A simple, satisfying tale, adorned and enlivened by these fine and spirited pictures. A good starting point for this author's work; totally unthreatening, with a nice touch of humor.

Jacob and Wilhelm Grimm collected German fairy stories in the early nineteenth century. Only a few of their stories are suitable for very young children, but these few should not be missed. Suitable editions are given below.

(GB) *The Elves and the Shoemaker*   Katrin Brandt   (Bodley Head/Puffin paperback)
Enchanting illustrations grace this most-suitable-of-all Grimm stories for the very young. The poor shoemaker and his wife are so grateful for the help of the two night-visiting elves that they make them each a suit of clothes. (Were ever elves so fetchingly attired—or so full of joy at their good fortune?) Infinite care has been given to detail in these pictures, and yet freshness and vigor abound. Not to be missed.

The Fisherman and His Wife   Monika Laimgruber   (Greenwillow)

This is a well-told version of a famous story. The fisherman's wife is over ambitious, and forces her frightened husband to collaborate in her plans for wealth and glory. The tale is lengthy, though gripping, and will be loved by near-six-year-olds whose listening experience has been extensive and varied. The illustrations are brilliant; framed, panoramic spreads demonstrate this artist's capacity to use color and line to striking and dramatic effect.

Hans in Luck   Felix Hoffmann   (Atheneum)

Lucky Hands   ed. Elizabeth Rose, illus. Gerald Rose   (Faber)
Simple, trusting Hans, on his way home with his wages (a lump of gold in the first version, silver in the second) is easily tricked into the long series of exchanges which leave him with nothing— except his happiness, and a loving welcome at home. Hans's adventures are shown in very clear detail against a white background in Hoffmann's version, an almost "comic strip" device which makes this mild and funny story accessible to the very young. The Roses's version has a comical good cheer about its clear, bright pages, which is very refreshing.

King Grisly-Beard   Maurice Sendak   (Farrar, Strauss & Giroux)

King Thrushbeard   Felix Hoffmann   (Harcourt Brace Jovanovich)
Very differently illustrated editions of the same story. Sendak's prince and princess are squat, square, humorously presented characters (ostensibly, children acting in a play). Hoffmann's treatment, while unusual, shows this artist's superb feeling for atmosphere and his usual technical brilliance. Both versions are for the upper experience level among the five-to-sixes.

Mother Holly   Bernadette Watts   (T. Y. Crowell)
Glowing illustrations make this large-format picture book a joy to handle. The story has all the elements of the folk tale without any of its darker features; a beautiful, industrious daughter and an

ugly, lazy one; a quest, with reward in gold for virtue, repetition
... and a happy ending.

(GB) *Rumpelstiltskin* Illus. William Stobbs (Bodley Head)
This is one of the most vivacious and vigorous of all Grimm's
stories. The little man who helped the miller's daugher spin straw
to gold and in return proposed to take her first child unless she
could guess his name, has always exerted fascination. Stobbs's
interpretation is hearty rather than frightening, humorous rather
than tragic. An entertaining, sure-footed production.

The Seven Ravens Felix Hoffmann (Harcourt Brace Jovanovich)
A haunting, beautiful story with the happiest of all endings "And
they all went joyfully home together." Here is deep feeling, great
dignity and real simplicity. Hoffmann is unsurpassed as an illustrator of fairy stories. In *The Seven Ravens* we see him at his
best.

(GB) *The Sleeping Beauty* Felix Hoffmann (Oxford)

(GB) *Briar Rose, the story of the Sleeping Beauty* Margery
Gill (Bodley Head)
Two very differently illustrated versions. Hoffmann's apparently
restrained but deeply feeling pictures, in muted, somber color,
contrast with Gill's vivid color and more earthly approach. Children who are ready for the suspense and wonder of this old story
will enjoy both forms.

(GB) *The Wolf and the Seven Little Kids* Felix Hoffmann (Oxford)
One of the most successful of all Grimm's stories for the fours
and fives, and certainly the most exuberant. In this landscape
sized book Hoffmann has scope for his virtuosity. The result is
full-blooded, tongue-in-cheek humor laced with hand-over-
mouth terror—with an assurance of doom for the wolf and triumph for the goat family. Almost unbelievably good, in all ways.

Joseph Jacobs is a famous name in the storytelling world. Most of his work was done in the second half of the last century. The following two titles make a good introduction.

(GB) *The Crock of Gold*   William Stobbs   (Bodley Head)
This is the famous story of the Pedlar of Swaffham, who travelled to London to find riches and made a strange discovery. The illustrations are striking in their brilliant color and landscape design. A simple version, which introduces the child to unfamiliar, but easily understood expressions, "but naught did he see and naught did he hear."

Hereafterthis   Paul Galdone   (McGraw-Hill)
The classic story of the simple farmer and his even more simple wife, who, between them, almost (but not quite) lose all their wealth and worldly goods to a band of robbers. The thieves are robust rather than evil, and good humor is the keynote. The pictures complement the rollicking text exactly. They are bright in color and full of vigorous, earthy humor.

Fables are short stories with morals, or lessons, implied. Although they are usually simple in construction and language, they require some maturity of understanding.

Aesop is the most famous of all fable writers. The following, among his tales, are suitable for young children. Each has a simple theme, and colorful, spirited illustrations.

The Hare and the Frogs   William Stobbs   (Bodley Head)

Wolf! Wolf!   Elizabeth and Gerald Rose   (Faber)

La Fontaine, a French collector of fables has inspired Brian Wildsmith to produce picture books of startling beauty. In rich, glowing color, with simple—even sparse—text, these are joyful books; each a thing of beauty.

The Hare and the Tortoise
The Lion and the Rat
The Miller, the Boy and the Donkey
The North Wind and the Sun
The Rich Man and the Shoe-maker   (all published by Oxford)

Conclusion

I hope that this book has gone some way towards convincing you that books are important for your baby and child, and for babies and children everywhere. I hope also that I have conveyed my reasons to you for my belief in books and given you a true picture of what I feel they can accomplish in the lives of young children.

A great deal is said and written these days about the need to speed up the learning process, to get children's minds ticking over at earlier and earlier ages. It can all sound very serious; quite out of touch with the joy, the bounce and the humor that is the real nature of childhood. Heaven forbid that I should have contributed to this over-sober view of a parent's role!

My hope for children is that they will learn to live richly and well; that each child will use his unique qualities to become a happy, contributing adult.

Every person in the world is unique, and every person is essentially alone. We cannot change this aloneness, but we can reduce its effects. Relationships are the key. We nourish our essential humanity when we make contact with one another.

Forging a close relationship with our own baby is easy.

Babies are totally unstinting in their willingness to accept us as fountains of pleasure and support. We will be immeasurably enriched by their uncritical devotion, and they, by our love, in return. But we need things in common. No relationship can survive on a basis of mutual, unquestioning adoration.

For relationships, minds have to engage. Ideas are essential, and books constitute a superlative source of ideas. Books can be bridges between children and parents, and children and the world.

There is one overriding requirement, however, if books are to work for children in this way. They have to be successful books, books that will make a child sit up and take notice, laugh, and ask "Why?". Books that will involve him deeply and lift him out of the here-and-now to a place of wonder. "Read it again" will always be the highest accolade. Such books exist. I hope that *this* book will help you to find some of them and identify others, and that your own developing relationship with your child will keep you reading them together.